CINCINNATI SYMPHONY ORCHESTRA

CENTENNIAL PORTRAITS

1 9 9 4

PUBLISHED BY THE CINCINNATI SYMPHONY ORCHESTRA

*The production of CENTENNIAL PORTRAITS
was made possible through a generous grant from*

STAR BANK

with significant contributions from:
The Hennegan Company
Sam Ashworth Design
RIS Paper Co.

*Special thanks to all those who contributed
photographs and documents for the Centennial
Celebration and to the following organizations and
individuals for their help toward the production of
CENTENNIAL PORTRAITS:*
CSO Staff
Cecie Chewning
Mary Taylor
Cincinnati Historical Society
Linda Bailey
David Conzett
Charlotte E. Flanagan
Steve Wright
Cincinnati Enquirer
Ray Zwick
The Hennegan Company
Vicki Polanco
Barbara Runde
Susan Huthmann

CENTENNIAL PORTRAITS STAFF
Creative Director: Sam Ashworth
Introduction: Robert C. Vitz
Caption Editor: Francesca Norberg
Photography Editor: Sam Ashworth
Montage Photographs: John Gerhardstein
Contributors: Dianne Cooper
Dan Croft
Nellie Cummins

**The Corbett Foundation,
Centennial Celebration Sponsor**

ISBN 0-9643686-0-9

Printed in the United States by
The Hennegan Company.
Bound by C.J. Krehbiel Co.

C O N T E N T S

FOREWARD — 7

INTRODUCTION — 9

THE 1890s — 18

FRANK VAN DER STUCKEN 1895-1907 — 20

THE 1900s — 30

LEOPOLD STOKOWSKI 1909-1912 — 32

THE 1910s — 42

ERNST KUNWALD 1912-1917 — 44

THE 1920s — 54

EUGÉNE YSAŸE 1918-1922 — 56

THE 1930s — 66

FRITZ REINER 1922-1931 — 68

THE 1940s — 78

EUGENE GOOSSENS 1931-1947 — 80

THE 1950s — 90

THOR JOHNSON 1947-1958 — 92

THE 1960s — 102

MAX RUDOLF 1958-1969 — 104

THE 1970s — 114

THOMAS SCHIPPERS 1970-1977 — 116

THE 1980s — 126

MICHAEL GIELEN 1980-1986 — 128

THE 1990s — 138

JESÚS LÓPEZ-COBOS 1986 - PRESENT — 140

CINCINNATI SYMPHONY ORCHESTRA — 150

DISCOGRAPHY — 152

CENTENNIAL COMMITTEES — 155

BIBLIOGRAPHY — 156

HISTORY — 158

PHOTOGRAPHY CREDITS — 160

F O R E W A R D

It is my great pleasure and a special honor to be Music Director of the Cincinnati Symphony Orchestra in this, its Centennial Season. The Cincinnati Symphony Orchestra is only the fifth American orchestra to reach the centennial milestone. This auspicious occasion presents a wonderful opportunity to explore the history of the Orchestra, from its early role as an extension of the European (and especially German) community to its present-day stature as one of the nation's leading orchestras. The early traditions have been kept alive while the CSO has evolved, along with the city of Cincinnati, to become wholly American.

This book will guide you through the eras of each of the CSO's past ten music directors with a fascinating array of photographs and commentary. Trace the orchestra's early beginnings under Frank Van der Stucken, through generations of American history and up to the present day. Discover the relationship between the CSO and legendary composers and performers. Become acquainted with the men and women of both the past and present, whose support and commitment helped to make this Centennial Season celebration a reality.

One of our goals for the future is to examine the CSO's role in the community, to insure that the Orchestra will be cherished and enjoyed for another 100 years. We can all be proud of the prestige which the CSO has brought to this city, and I would like to thank the wonderful people of Cincinnati for their support. Without each and every one of you, the CSO could not maintain the highest possible level of quality.

I hope you enjoy this journey through the CSO's first 100 years, and can be with us as we begin to write the next chapter of the history of the Cincinnati Symphony Orchestra.

Jesús López-Cobos
Music Director

The Cincinnati Orchestra Association Company.

—DIRECTORS—

Mrs. Wm. H. Taft, *Pres't.*
Mrs. E. K. Stallo, *First Vice-Pres't.*
Mrs. Louise N. Anderson, *Second Vice-Pres't.*
Miss S. H. Woolley, *Secretary.*
Mrs. F. Forchheimer, *Corresponding Sec'y.*
Miss Isabel Jelke, *Treasurer.*
Mrs. A. H. Chatfield. Mrs. Henriette Billing.

Mrs. Clifford B. Wright.
Mrs. Louis N. Stix.
Mrs. Lawrence Poland.
Mrs. Charles P. Taft.
Miss Emma Roedter.
Mrs. Joseph Wilby.
Mrs. C. R. Holmes.

Cincinnati, May——————, 1894.

M————————————————————
————————————————————

The Cincinnati Orchestra Association Company has been incorporated under the laws of the State of Ohio, for the purpose of providing a permanent orchestra of a high standard for Cincinnati.

In all the musical history of this city no time is more opportune than the present for the consideration of this matter, which to be secured must receive the loyal co-operation of all our musical forces. Our city has long ranked as the leading musical center of the West, but there is danger of this distinction being lost.

To fulfill successfully our aim will require a director of the highest talent, and a number of competent musicians, necessitating the payment of a large amount of money for salaries.

As it will take a long time to make such an orchestra self-supporting, and as the capital of the Association is limited, we appeal to the patriotic citizens of Cincinnati to assist us in this undertaking. A large sum annually for the term of three years has already been subscribed, but much more will be required before the orchestra can be placed on a permanent footing. A subscription of Five Dollars ($5.00) a year for one or more years will entitle you to be placed on the list of contributing members.

The benefits arising to our city from such an orchestra can not be overestimated. The fact that it would be and remain distinctly a Cincinnati affair, should enable it to receive support here and from the towns tributary to us; and to the business interest, the fact that the money spent in support of a permanent orchestra would remain and be spent here, should be a matter of no small import. An orchestra harmoniously supported on the lines indicated, would give us yearly a series of concerts of a high degree of artistic excellence, which, with the aid of distinguished soloists, would form also a most attractive feature of social life.

In view of the many benefits to be gained by the establishment of this orchestra in our midst, we appeal to you to help our cause by a subscription, which will be repaid you many times in the benefits financial, social and artistic, which will accrue to Cincinnati.

Very respectfully yours,

Mrs. Albert H. Chatfield,
Mrs. Briggs Cunningham,
Mrs. N. Du Brul,
Mrs. Fred. Eckstein,
Mrs. Frank Ellis,
Miss Laura Glenn,
Miss Eda Kuhn,
Mrs. Hugo Kupferschmidt,
Mrs. Lawrence Poland,
Mrs. Jos. Ransohoff,
Miss Emma Roedter,
Miss Marie Schwill,
Miss Jennie S. Smith.

Mrs. Edmund K. Stallo,
Mrs. Louis N. Stix,
Miss Alice Sterne,
Mrs. Chas. P. Taft,
Mrs. Clifford B. Wright,
Mrs. Thos. Wood,
Mrs. E. Gustav Zinke,
Mr. Joseph L. Adler,
Mr. Howard Douglass,
Mr. Louis Ehrgott,
Mr. Edward Goepper,
Mr. Frank A. Lee,

Helen Herron Taft was the first president of the Cincinnati Orchestra Association.

One could have excused Frank Van der Stucken if he viewed the opening ceremony for the Cincinnati Symphony Orchestra's first concert with some puzzlement. As he waited to take the podium on that January evening in 1895, a trio of distinguished civic leaders – William Howard Taft, Melville E. Ingalls and A. Howard Hinkle – presented opening remarks to the modest audience at Pike's Opera House on Fourth Street. Yet, as Van der Stucken well knew, the force behind the orchestra's founding had come from the Ladies Musical Club, a group of musically inclined and socially prominent women, who had established the Cincinnati Orchestra Association the previous year, with Helen Herron Taft (Mrs. William Howard Taft) as its president. Indeed, it had been Mrs. Taft who had been the Texas-born director's most enthusiastic supporter, but in polite circles tradition still discouraged public appearances by women. Thus, the men, who had provided considerable financial and emotional support, attended to the honors.

That this group of women, devoted "to the study and practice of music and the promotion of a higher musical taste and culture," founded the Cincinnati Symphony Orchestra is virtually unique in the history of this country's artistic institutions. What circumstances led to this triumph of female leadership? How had these women usurped the male presence that dominated the city's other cultural endeavors? The answer is, of course, that they usurped nothing. The men had simply abdicated their position.

The roots of the CSO extend deep into Cincinnati's past. During its early years the city had experienced the musical activities of fast growing, ambitious frontier communities: active church choirs, successful programs by touring performers, a scattering of usually short-lived music schools, and even, for a time, a local orchestra. But if musical development commanded little real distinction, the city's reputation grew in other ways. Artists such as Worthington Whittredge, Hiram Powers, Robert S. Duncanson and James H. Beard gave Cincinnati a well deserved reputation as a regional art center, and this, coupled with a handful of minor literary figures and several active intellectual societies, led some admirers to call the city the "Athens of the West."

For a community scarcely sixty years removed from the wilderness, Cincinnati's future looked remarkably secure by mid-century. Population had soared to 115,000, making it the sixth largest city in the nation. Situated on the largest river system of the continent, tied by a canal(s) to the Great Lakes, and surrounded by bountiful farmland, rapid commercial and industrial growth appeared certain. Henry Longfellow had paid poetic tribute in describing the city as "The Queen of the West, in her garlands dressed," and Cincinnatians proudly adopted the title. Already larger than any of its western rivals, local boosters projected the city some day to rival New York in size and influence. The boisterous public landing, with its scores of steamboats and endless profusion of goods, mirrored the city's prosperity. A phalanx of solid brick buildings fronted Second and Third streets; impressive homes anchored the eastern and western edges of the tightly clustered community, with a few mansions already dotting the hilltops; but most representative of the city's importance was the just-opened six-story Burnet House, one of the great hotels of its day, the imposing dome of which challenged the many church steeples for supremacy of the skyline.

In the midst of this half raw, half refined development came the stream of German immigrants who provided Cincinnati with its first real musical distinction. Arriving in ever growing numbers after 1835, both by choice and by prejudice, these hearty newcomers congregated in the area across the recently completed Miami and Erie Canal, soon to be known by all as "Over the Rhine," where a transplanted culture quickly emerged. The German love of music produced a cultural leavening that shaped the city for decades. Bands and singing societies sprouted, leading quickly to outdoor summer festivals where in a relaxed atmosphere of food and drink the Germans enjoyed old country fellowship. In 1849 local singing groups invited their counterparts from nearby communities to participate in a *saengerfest*, a three day gathering of *Gemütlichkeit* and song. Success led to the establishment of the *NordAmerikanischer Saengerbund* and annual musical gatherings that for the next forty years rotated among the principal western cities. As they did in most American cities, Germans came to dominate Cincinnati's musical development.

In the years just prior to the outbreak of the Civil War, two men in particular advanced the cause of serious music. Frederic Ritter, only 22 years old but born and trained in Europe, brought his unbridled enthusiasm to Cincinnati in 1856. In short order he organized the Cecelia Society, comprised of both German and non-German singers, and established the city's second attempt at an orchestra, the Cincinnati Philharmonic, made up of twenty-six local German musicians. Under Ritter's direction the Philharmonic introduced Cincinnatians to a Teutonic diet of Mozart, Beethoven, Haydn, and even Wagner. Despite favorable comments in several of the city's newspapers, Ritter's vision exceeded the realities of the day. Never able to expand the orchestra's size or find sufficient financial support, the Philharmonic was almost moribund when Ritter left in 1861. Into the breach left by Ritter's departure stepped the Silesian-born Carl Barus. Active among German choral groups since his arrival in 1851, Barus, who took over leadership of both the Cecelia Society and the Philharmonic, carried forward the city's musical life for the next decade. Although the Philharmonic continued to struggle, finally succumbing in 1868, the community's choral tradition remained vital, strengthened in the mid-1860s by the Harmonic Society, an organization dominated by some of the city's most prosperous non-Germans.

However, the Civil War was not kind to cultural endeavors, siphoning time, money and energy away from the arts. Nor were the arts the only noticeable area of decline in the Queen City. Observers pointed out that the city's growth rate had slipped since the 1840s, that economic indicators now favored western rivals Chicago and St. Louis, and that the city had taken on a dowdy appearance. One concerned resident described the downtown as "standing still." What seemed to

Frederic Ritter

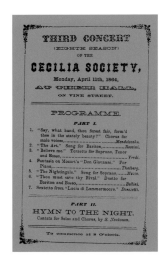

Theodore Thomas

define Cincinnati to many visitors were the ever present coal smoke and the unpleasant odors emanating from the stockyards. In response to these concerns a new public spirit gradually emerged in the late 1860s. The city initiated a series of highly successful industrial expositions, laid the groundwork for a direct railroad connection to the South, and made plans for opening the surrounding hilltops by constructing inclined planes. In 1871 residents celebrated the magnificant Tyler Davidson Fountain, a gift of Henry Probasco. The same year McMicken College, a gift of Charles McMicken, opened its doors, and Andrew Erkenbrecher proposed a zoological garden. In the midst of this civic energy, local Germans brought the 1870 *Saengerfest* to Cincinnati. It was an enormous undertaking. To accommodate the anticipated throngs, the city constructed a two-story facility between Elm Street and the canal (where Music Hall stands today) on the western edge of the German district. Two hundred and fifty feet long and one hundred and ten feet wide, the hastily built *Saengerhalle* could accommodate 3000 singers and musicians, along with 10,000 listeners. In keeping with the Teutonic flavor, the lower level was reserved for food and drink.

Eighteen hundred singers, representing 61 societies from around the region, and an orchestra of 75 provided the musical fare. Opening day brought forth flower-strewn and flag-bedecked streets, a two and one-half hour parade of enthusiastic performers, and extensive coverage in both English and German daily newspapers. Governor Rutherford B. Hayes, himself a former resident of the city, gave the opening address. The four-day event, which opened with Handel's "Hallelujah Chorus," appealed to the entire community and brought to the city its first national recognition.

A less noticeable but equally powerful musical force had reached Cincinnati a year earlier. Theodore Thomas, a German-born but largely American-reared musician, decided to take his New York-based orchestra on a national tour. The Queen City was one of his stops. Although this first appearance drew only 200 listeners to Mozart Hall, Thomas discovered to his surprise "excellent choral societies and an orchestra [Carl Barus'] superior to that of any city west of New York." The Thomas orchestra returned each year, and each year audiences grew.

Saengerhalle

George Ward Nichols

REUBEN R. SPRINGER

Due to the overwhelming success of the first two May Festivals, Cincinnati found itself in need of a more suitable facility in which to hold these events. Local businessman Reuben Springer took the initiative by donating $125,000 toward the construction of a music hall, with the condition that the city provide a suitable lot and the citizens of Cincinnati match his gift. The grand structure was built on the site of the former Saengerhalle and was completed in 1878.

As he was doing throughout the country, Theodore Thomas cultivated and developed musical appreciation, especially for the German symphonic tradition. His unerring taste, orchestral discipline, and devotion to an increasingly all classical program paid dividends, especially in reaching the primarily Anglo-Saxon, upper class society. At the conclusion of his 1872 visit, Thomas, along with Maria Longworth Nichols and her husband, George Ward Nichols, sketched out plans for a major musical festival to be held the following year. This threesome sought a dignified celebration of the finest choral and orchestral music, and they consciously rejected both the flamboyant atmosphere of Patrick Gilmore's recent Boston Peace Jubilees and the heavily ethnic *Saengerfests*. With George Nichols handling the administrative details and Thomas the musical direction, Cincinnati's first May Festival astounded the nation. From the opening movement of Handel's *Dettingen Te Deum* to Beethoven's majestic Fifth Symphony, the 108-piece orchestra and 800-member chorus swept all before them. Newspapers from St. Louis to Boston sang the festival's praises. And while Thomas and most of his orchestra came from New York, local supporters praised most highly the chorus, which came largely from the city. Coming on top of the 1872 Liberal Republican presidential convention and the highly successful industrial expositions, the 1873 May Festival injected into the city a new sense of confidence.

The May Festivals became biannual events, each adding a new gem to the city's crown, and they triggered a succession of impressive musical advances in the city. Community support, led by Reuben R. Springer's generosity, underwrote the construction of Music Hall, the nation's finest concert hall when it opened in 1878. Two years later the College of Music, with Theodore Thomas as musical director and George Nichols as business manager, opened its doors in anticipation of becoming the premier music school in the country. City enthusiasts crowed. *Saengerfests*, the May Festivals, Music Hall, now Theodore Thomas...what more could the future bring? The editor of the *Cincinnati Daily Gazette* boasted that Cincinnati would soon become "the great musical center of the world," while others optimistically referred to the city as "the Paris of America." The euphoria was short-lived. Eighteen months after opening, the College of Music was in disarray. Trying to harness the imperious Thomas and the strong-willed Nichols proved nearly disasterous. Thomas had wanted an institution devoted to artistic excellence, while Nichols represented the board of directors' concern that the school be financially self-supporting. On paper the authority of each man appeared separate; in reality artistry and economics continually overlapped. In the Spring of 1880 a frustrated and angry Thomas resigned and returned to New York, leaving a residue of bitterness. Although Nichols took charge of the school, the loss to the city was devastating, for in one stroke the college's reputation had been reduced to regional claims.

There is no question that Cincinnati would have gained a permanent orchestra at least a decade earlier if Thomas had remained. Part of his assigned responsibility had been to establish a college orchestra, which he had done by absorbing most of the members of the 40-piece Cincinnati Grand Orchestra, organized in 1872 by Louis Ballenberg and George Brand. Given the national impetus at that time for symphony orchestras and Cincinnati's drive for musical recognition, the college orchestra would almost certainly have become such an organization. Instead, Thomas' abrupt departure split the local music community. Although the majority of local musicians took Thomas' side, several, including Simon Jacobsohn, principal violinist on the college faculty, and May Festival chorus director Otto Singer, publicly criticized Thomas. And when

The first opera festival in 1881 drew an opening night audience of 5,000 to Music Hall for a presentation of "Lohengrin."

Lucien Wulsin

14

Thomas then dismissed Singer from his May Festival position, the breach within the city's music community widened further.

The College of Music survived of course, but under Nichols' hand and, after his death in 1885, Peter R. Neff's, the school became identified with the anti-Thomas element in the city. The May Festival, which Thomas continued to direct until his death in 1905, carried the pro-Thomas banner. In an attempt to shore up its reputation and to compensate for its severance from the popular and profitable May Festivals, the college sponsored an opera festival in February 1881. The ambitious Nichols engaged Her Majesty's Opera Company, under the direction of James Mapleson, to perform seven operas in seven days, with Etelka Gerster, "the Hungarian Nightingale," as prima donna. In order to produce a festival "on a scale of magnificence unparalleled in this country or in Europe," Music Hall was refurbished with special satin and gold boxes, a new curtain, and a proscenium for the stage. Five thousand opera lovers filled the auditorium for the lavish opening of *Lohengrin*, with standing room seats selling for one dollar. The seldom modest Mapleson called it "the most daring musical enterprise ever attempted in America or any other country." Hyperbole aside, critics found much to praise. In each of the next two years the college sponsored even more successful festivals, including one with a performance in *Aida* by the celebrated Adelina Patti, for which almost 7,000 people jammed Music Hall. However, the 1884 festival fell on hard times. A flooding Ohio River kept attendance down, and for the first time the college lost money. Nichols' declining health and death the following year ended the brief series.

Indeed, the difficulties of the last opera festival served as a portent for the rest of the decade. Cincinnati's musical fortunes steadily deteriorated. If the decade of the seventies had witnessed unqualified success, in the eighties Orpheus seemed to have forgotten the city. Although the May Festivals retained their excellence, if not their novelty, they generated less enthusiasm and interest; and the poison from the Thomas-Singer rift continued to impede attempts at other musical endeavors. Without Theodore Thomas and his supporters the college could not maintain its orchestra. Many of the musicians then helped reorganize the Cincinnati Grand Orchestra, and Lucien Wulsin, president of the Musical Club and a partner in the D. H. Baldwin Co., tried to line up backers for a short concert season in 1881. Support could not be found. Similar attempts in 1882 and 1883 met the same fate. In 1884 Wulsin and Peter R. Neff, soon to head the College of Music, reorganized the Cincinnati Grand Orchestra as the Philharmonic Orchestra, under Michael Brand's direction. That autumn a short but successful season gave hope that the city had at last weathered its musical storms. The cooperation of Wulsin, a May Festival Association board member, and Neff, of the College of Music, provided an opportunity to heal the wounds, but harmony dissolved the next year in a challenge to Brand's leadership. Brand resigned, and three violinists competed for the vacant position. This re-kindled old antagonisms, and the heated competition led to an uncomfortable joint directorship of John Broeckhoven and Henry Schradieck; the third candidate, Simon Jacobsohn, "drew off in a huff."

The Philharmonic struggled financially, and within several years the College of Music had to take control over it, restoring for a short time the school's orchestral training role. In its first season as the college orchestra, Schradieck presented an uninspiring series of concerts. The orchestra broke up shortly. Paralleling the demise of the Philharmonic, the May Festival wrestled with internal problems. The Court House riot of 1884 cut into ticket sales and led to the organization's first deficit, and growing opposition to Thomas' handling of

Michael Brand

the May Festival Chorus led to Lucien Wulsin's resignation from the Festival board, ending the link between the rival factions the Philharmonic had forged. Even the Grand Orchestra, revived once again by Michael Brand, had deserted serious music for more profitable popular concerts. When a local reporter took issue with the orchestra's musical selections, Brand bitterly replied, "We give the people what they like. They don't want anything better." By the end of the eighties, musical life in the city had faded to pleasant but undemanding performances, band concerts in the parks, and student or faculty recitals at the College of Music or Clara Baur's Conservatory of Music. Cincinnati's pretensions of musical supremacy had collapsed. The final blow fell when Chicago gleefully announced in 1891 that it had secured Theodore Thomas to develop its symphony orchestra.

Into this state of affairs stepped the Ladies Musical Club, established in 1891. After sponsoring several concerts, including a well attended performance by the Boston Symphony Orchestra, the women looked to larger goals. Recognizing that old antagonisms were at last receding, the club set out to establish a symphony orchestra for the city. Although by birth and marriage, these women represented many prominent Cincinnati families, they determined at the outset to maintain control of the Orchestra Association, limiting men to supportive roles. Harnessing love of music with a new burst of civic spirit, they succeeded in raising the necessary money from local business and professional leaders. The best local musicians eagerly joined the new orchestra, but the selection of a director almost proved fatal to the fledgling organization. To avoid bringing up "old feuds," the board of directors opted for an outsider. Calling on Theodore Thomas, New York (and former Cincinnati) music critic Henry Krehbiel, Charles Ellis of the Boston Symphony Orchestra, and Walter Damrosch of the New York Philharmonic Orchestra for suggestions, the board eventually focused on two names, Frank Van der Stucken and Henry Schradieck. Schradieck, active in Cincinnati in the mid-1880s, had just recently returned from several years of study in Europe, while the relatively unknown Van der Stucken had directed the Arion Society of New York for the past ten years. Complicating the selection process was the Orchestra Association's desire to have the new director also direct the May Festivals as a way of further uniting the community, a situation eventually blocked by the May Festival president. After failing to reach an agreement with Van der Stucken in the summer of 1894, the Orchestra Association launched a makeshift concert season with musical direction divided among Van der Stucken, Schradieck and Anton Seidl, a prominent Wagnerian enthusiast. Each one was to conduct three concerts, with Van der Stucken to lead off in January, followed by Seidl and Schradieck in subsequent months. Since Seidl was not interested in the position, the concert season served to keep Van der Stucken's candidacy alive while appeasing Schradieck's supporters on the board. However, when the Texan took the podium for the first performance, the general enthusiasm for his direction led Mrs. Taft to open negotiations with him. Just days before Schradieck mounted the stage for his April concerts, Van der Stucken signed a six year contract. The Cincinnati Symphony Orchestra was on its way.

Robert C. Vitz

Frank Van der Stucken

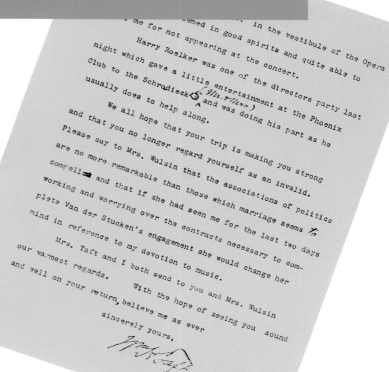

United States
Circuit Court of Appeals.
For the Sixth Circuit.
Judges Chambers.
Cincinnati.

April 12th. 1895

Lucien Wulsin ,Esq.

   c/o Monroe & Co.
   7 Rue Scribe

   Paris, France

My Dear Lucien:---

        Enclosed you will find a contract between Van der Stucken, yourself as trustee and Mr. Schmidlapp as treasurer, which Mr. Schmidlapp signed for you as trustee and for himself as treasurer. Mr.Schmidlapp in a letter to Van der Stucken guaranteed that you would ratify this signature. To comply with this guaranty,I herewith enclose a form to be signed by you with a copy of the contract as signed attached. Will you kindly sign the same and send it to Van der Stucken to his European address which is given below? The guaranty a copy of which is contained in the contract was drawn by Mr. Ingalls to suit his views. I drew the contract between Van der Stucken and yourself and Mr. Schmidlapp to conform as near as might be to the guaranty. This explains my having anything to do with the matter. Mr. Schmidlapp proposes

in the vestibule of the Opera seemed in good spirits and quite able to me for not appearing at the concert.

Harry Roelker was one of the directors party last night which gave a little entertainment at the Phoenix Club to the Schradieck (Mr. Ylur) and was doing his part as he usually does to help along.

We all hope that your trip is making you strong and that you no longer regard yourself as an invalid. Please say to Mrs. Wulsin that the associations of politics are no more remarkable than those which marriage seems to compel and that if she had seen me for the last two days working and worrying over the contracts necessary to complete Van der Stucken's engagement she would change her mind in reference to my devotion to music.

Mrs. Taft and I both send to you and Mrs. Wulsin our warmest regards. With the hope of seeing you sound and well on your return, believe me as ever

      sincerely yours,

      Wm. H. Taft.

F. van der Stucken

126

20

FRANK VAN DER STUCKEN

–––––––– 1895 - 1907 ––––––––

The first permanent conductor of the Cincinnati Symphony Orchestra was Frank Van der Stucken. Born in Fredericksburg, Texas, October 15, 1858, of Belgian-German parentage, Van der Stucken was thirty-seven when he assumed conductorship of the CSO. He received his musical training in Europe, including instruction in composition by Edvard Grieg. Upon his return to the United States in 1884, Van der Stucken succeeded Leopold Damrosch as conductor of the Arion Society of New York, a post he continued until his move to Cincinnati.

Beginning with only 48 musicians, Van der Stucken presented the usual fare of German, Belgian and French music. Gradually he enlarged the orchestra to 60 and expanded the repertoire to include the works of American composers George Chadwick, Arthur Foote, Victor Herbert and Edward MacDowell. His musical duties were increased when in 1895 Van der Stucken was offered the Directorship of the Cincinnati College of Music, a post he retained until 1903.

In 1906 Van der Stucken assumed directorship of the May Festival and the Cincinnati Symphony Orchestra became the "house orchestra" for these presentations, a commission it still fulfills today. Van der Stucken continued this post with the May Festival until 1912 after relinquishing his position as CSO conductor in 1907.

At the end of the 1906-07 season, Van der Stucken was greeted warmly by audiences at his final concerts. He was praised in the community for his efforts in developing the new orchestra into a first-rate musical organization through his disciplined approach to rehearsals and imaginative programming. After moving to Europe, Van der Stucken continued to compose and conduct until his death in 1929.

*Cincinnati Symphony
Orchestra under the direction
of assistant conductor
Michael Brand, whose
Cincinnati Grand Orchestra
formed the nucleus of the new
orchestra, ca. 1895.*

Pike's Opera House, on Fourth Street between Vine and Walnut, was the symphony's home for the first two seasons. Built in 1859 by distiller Samuel N. Pike, the opera house was the finest concert hall west of Philadelphia and the center of Cincinnati entertainment until it burned to the ground in 1866. It was rebuilt by Pike in 1871 only to be destroyed again by fire in 1903.

CINCINNATI SYMPHONY ORCHESTRA
Personnel - 1895 Program Listing

FIRST VIOLINS
Schmitt, H., Principal
Froehlich, H.
Eich, H.
Hahn, A.
Kupferschmid, H.
Schath, A.
Eisen, C.
Weigand, L.
Theill, E.

SECOND VIOLINS
Peters, A.
Esberger, M.
Schehl, J.
Schath, G.
Bohrer, J.
Woest, A.
Brand, Al.

VIOLAS
Stuempel, F.
Brand, Ar.
Reinhart, C.
Burckhardt, G.

VIOLONCELLOS
Brand, M.
Kopp, H.
Hahn, C.
Zwissler, E.

DOUBLE BASSES
Menge, R.
Burck, H.
Liebholdt, A.
Weiss, F.

HARP
Mrs. Lawrence

FLUTES
Hahn, T.
Weber, L.

PICCOLO
Loehmann, G.

OBOES
Ross, W.
Dothe, H.

ENGLISH HORN
Ross, W.

CLARINETS
Schuett, C.
Schath, H.

BASSOON
Woest, H.

HORNS
Schrickel, A.
Bernhardt, C.
Knauft, A.

TUBA
Bruggeman, P.

TRUMPETS
Bellstedt, H.
Kopp, W.
Sievers, H.

TROMBONES
Kohlmann, C.
Brand, L.
Brand, G.

TYMPANI
Brand, Leo

SMALL DRUM
Brand, Al.

BASS DRUM
Bartsch, A.

LIBRARIAN
Brand, Leo

On January 17, 1895, after just a few rehearsals, the Cincinnati Symphony Orchestra opened its debut concert with a performance of Mozart's Symphony in G Minor. The concert was received with high praise and optimism as Cincinnati looked to a new century.

EDITOR'S NOTE:
Each orchestra roster was reproduced as it originally appeared in the first program for each music director's tenure.

EDITOR'S NOTE:
Shown above is an advertisement from the first CSO concert program in 1895. Advertisements from other programs are reproduced throughout the book.

Front on Elm Street, 402 feet.
Depth, 316 "
Height, 150 "

CINCINNATI MUSIC HALL AND EXPO

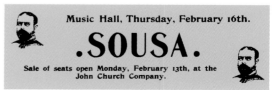
26

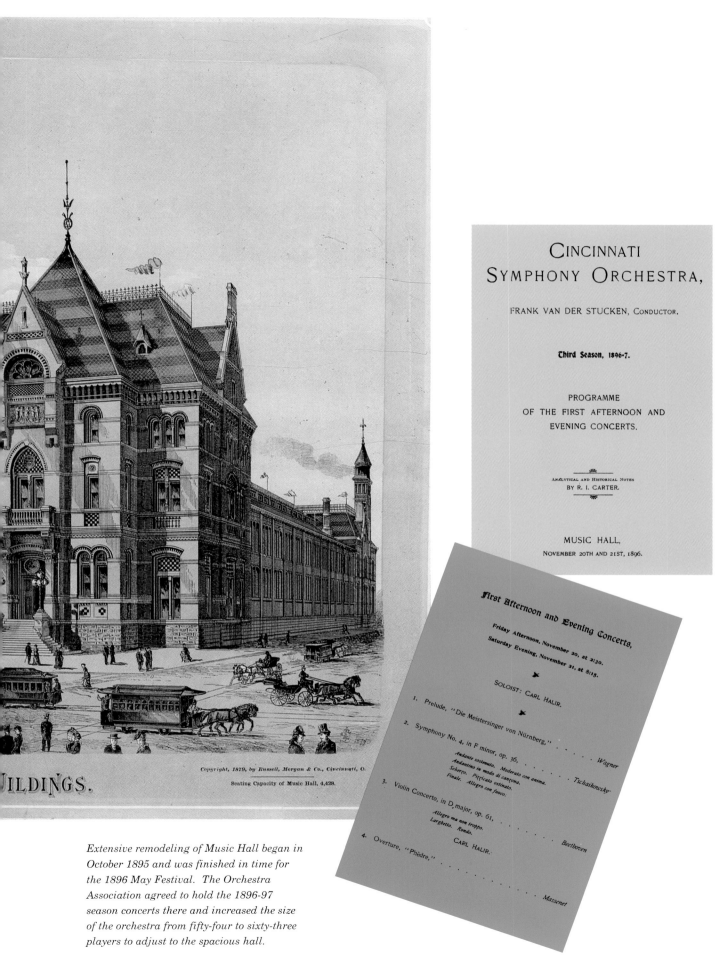

UILDINGS.

Copyright, 1879, by Russell, Morgan & Co., Cincinnati, O.

Seating Capacity of Music Hall, 4,428.

Extensive remodeling of Music Hall began in October 1895 and was finished in time for the 1896 May Festival. The Orchestra Association agreed to hold the 1896-97 season concerts there and increased the size of the orchestra from fifty-four to sixty-three players to adjust to the spacious hall.

Violin virtuoso Fritz Kreisler was one of the first world-renowned guest soloists to appear with the Cincinnati Symphony Orchestra. His 1901 appearance was the first of many with the CSO.

The Orchestra, which began its regional touring efforts in 1902, is shown leaving on a 1904 tour.

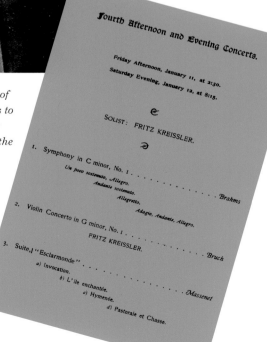

Fourth Afternoon and Evening Concerts.

Friday Afternoon, January 11, at 2:30.
Saturday Evening, January 12, at 8:15.

SOLIST: FRITZ KREISSLER.

1. Symphony in C minor, No. 1 . . . . Brahms
    Un poco sostenuto, Allegro.
    Andante sostenuto.
    Allegretto.
    Adagio, Andante, Allegro.

2. Violin Concerto in G minor, No. 1 . . . . Bruch
    FRITZ KREISSLER.

3. Suite, "Esclarmonde" . . . . Massenet
    a) Invocation.
    b) L'ile enchantée.
    c) Hymenée.
    d) Pastorale et Chasse.

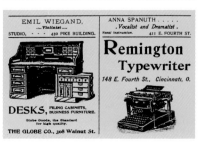
28

Tenth Concerts.

FRIDAY AFTERNOON, APRIL 8, AT 2:30.

SATURDAY EVENING, APRIL 9, AT 8:15.

Conductors: DR. RICHARD STRAUSS,
FRANK VAN DER STUCKEN.

SOLOIST: MME. PAULINE STRAUSS-DE AHNA.

Program.

Symphony in E minor, No. 5. .... *Peter Ilytsh Tschaïkowsky*

Tone Poem, "Don Juan," Opus 20 .... *Richard Strauss*

Songs with orchestra:

   (*a*) "Das Rosenband," Opus 36, No. 1.

   (*b*) "Liebeshymnus."

   (*c*) "Morgen," Opus 27, No. 4.   .... *Richard Strauss*

   (*d*) "Caecilie," Opus 27, No. 2.

Tone Poem, "Tod und Verklärung," Opus 24 .... *Richard Strauss*

STEINWAY PIANO USED.

Famed composer and conductor Richard Strauss led the CSO in his own works during the 1903-1904 season, with his wife Pauline de Ahna Strauss appearing as vocal soloist. Strauss' compositions were also championed by later CSO music directors, notably Ernst Kunwald and Fritz Reiner.

In 1905, the Cincinnati Symphony Orchestra under Music Director Frank Van der Stucken, performed the American premiere of Gustav Mahler's Symphony No. 5.

Ninth Concert.

SOLOIST: MME. BLOOMFIELD ZEISLER.

FRIDAY AFTERNOON, MARCH 24, AT 2:30.

SATURDAY EVENING, MARCH 25, AT 8.15.

Program.

Symphony No. 5 C Sharp Minor   *Gustav Mahler*
    (New, first time in America.)
            PART I.

  I.   Funeral March. (In gemessenem Schritt. Streng. Wie
       ein Konduct.) C-sharp minor.
  II.   Stormily restless   With utmost vehemence. (Stürmisch.
       bewegt. Mit grösster Vehemenz.) A minor.
            PART II.

 III   Scherzo. (Kräftig, nicht zu schnell.) D major.
            PART III.

 IV.   Adagietto (Sehr langsam.) F major.
  V.   Rondo—Finale. (Allegro.) D major.

Concerto for Piano, F minor, Op. 16   .   .   .   .   .   *Henselt*

Kaisermarsch   *Wagner*

STEINWAY GRAND PIANO USED.

For the reason that encores tend to impair the artistic unity of a given program, and further that many supporters of the Orchestra have asked that out-of-town patrons should not be inconvenienced by thus unduly prolonging the programs, the Board of Directors has decided to permit but one encore provided the soloist is willing.

LEOPOLD STOKOWSKI

—— 1909 - 1912 ——

From 1907 to 1909 the Cincinnati Symphony Orchestra was beset with labor and financial troubles and concerts by the local group were discontinued. The 1907-08 season was covered by visiting orchestras from Chicago, Pittsburgh, Boston and the New York Symphony and Russian Orchestra of New York, each performing a pair of concerts. The 1908-09 season was barren, however, as the Orchestra Association decided to devote their efforts to campaigning for the re-establishment of the CSO through the raising of a guaranty fund.

After securing the necessary funds to present a season of concerts in 1909-10, the Orchestra Board turned its attention to the matter of finding a new conductor. The name most often mentioned was that of twenty-seven year old Leopold Stokowski.

Born in London in 1882, Stokowski had begun his musical training as a child and continued further study at Queen's College and the Paris Conservatoire. At the time of his consideration for the CSO post, he was the organist-choirmaster at St. Bartholomew's Episcopal Church in New York.

In January of 1909 Stokowski's candidacy for the CSO position seemed to be in jeopardy. His lack of conducting experience and limited knowledge of the orchestral repertory were most frequently mentioned as drawbacks to his serious consideration as music director of what was becoming a major orchestral organization. But no one counted on Stokowski's determination and promotional abilities. Almost entirely through his creative correspondence to Board President Mrs. C. R. Holmes, the young man secured the position on a one-year contract.

Though brief, Leopold Stokowski's tenure as conductor and music director of the Cincinnati Symphony Orchestra could best be described as innovative and intense. During the next three years he increased the size of the orchestra to 77 men, experimented with orchestra seating arrangements for a better sound, and presented solid programming to increasingly enthusiastic audiences. In 1910, he initiated the first Pops Concerts and the next year increased the subscription concerts to twelve pairs. Then at the conclusion of the 1912 season, Stokowski abruptly announced his resignation. His developing flamboyant style had met head-on with the more conservative views of the Orchestra board and soon the "wonder child" was on his way to Philadelphia and future musical greatness.

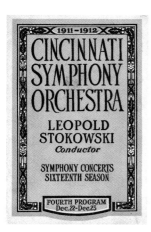

The first rehearsal of the Cincinnati Symphony Orchestra under the direction of 27-year old Leopold Stokowski, prior to their premiere concert on November 26, 1909. The photograph appeared in the Commercial Tribune and was the first commercially published photograph by Paul Briol, Cincinnati's first prominent photographer.

In January 1910, the celebrated Russian pianist Sergei Rachmaninoff performed his Second Piano Concerto for an enthusiastic Cincinnati audience. He appeared with the CSO again the following season and years later during the 1937-38 season under the baton of Eugene Goossens. In 1918, Rachmaninoff was offered the conductorship of the CSO but turned it down in favor of a career as a piano virtuoso.

Rachmaninoff

77

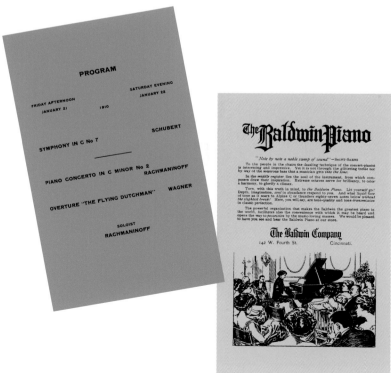

PROGRAM

FRIDAY AFTERNOON
JANUARY 21 1910

SATURDAY EVENING
JANUARY 22

SYMPHONY IN C No 7   SCHUBERT

PIANO CONCERTO IN C MINOR No 2   RACHMANINOFF

OVERTURE "THE FLYING DUTCHMAN"   WAGNER

SOLOIST
RACHMANINOFF

The Baldwin Piano

"Note by note a noble sweep of sound" — SAINT-SAENS

To the people in the chairs the dazzling technique of the concert-pianist is interesting and impressive. Yet it is not through the glittering treble nor by way of the sonorous bass that a musician gets *into the tone:*

In the *middle* register lies the soul of the instrument, from which composers draw their inspiration. Extreme octaves serve for brilliancy, to color a harmony, to glorify a climax.

Turn, with this truth in mind, to *the Baldwin Piano*. Let yourself go? Depth, imagination, *soul* in abundance respond to you. And what liquid flow of tone as it soars to Alpine C or thunders eighty-seven notes below *without the slightest break!* Here, you will say, are tone-quality and tone-transmission in classic perfection.

The powerful organization that makes the Baldwin the greatest piano in the world, facilitates also the convenience with which it may be heard and opens the way to possession by the music-loving masses. We would be pleased to have you see and hear the Baldwin Piano at our store.

The Baldwin Company
142 W. Fourth St.   Cincinnati.

In October 1908, in memory of her late husband, Thomas J. Emery, Mrs. Mary M. Emery donated $500,000 to the Ohio Mechanic's Institute for the construction of a five-story building which would include an assembly hall, suitable for lectures and concerts. The CSO Board had long expressed the desire for a smaller, more intimate concert hall, the 3,600 seat Music Hall being too vast for orchestra audiences at the time. The 2,211 seat Emery Auditorium was home for the Cincinnati Symphony Orchestra from 1912 until 1936.

IMPORTANT NOTICE

THE MANAGEMENT OF THE
CINCINNATI SYMPHONY ORCHESTRA
ASSOCIATION

Begs to announce that unless unforeseen delays occur, the concert of SATURDAY EVENING, JANUARY 6th, will be held in the new Emery Auditorium, Walnut Street above Canal. The concert of FRIDAY AFTERNOON, JANUARY 5th, will be given in Music Hall.

Patrons of concerts are asked to watch the newspapers for final information as to where the concert of SATURDAY EVENING, JANUARY 6th, will be held.

The newspapers will also contain notice of traffic regulations, etc.

PROGRAM

(FRENCH SCHOOL)

FRIDAY AFTERNOON JANUARY 5	1912	SATURDAY EVENING JANUARY 6

SYMPHONY IN D MINOR   CÉSAR FRANCK

    I. Lento: allegro non troppo.
    II. Allegretto.
    III. Allegro non troppo.

"L'APRÉS-MIDI D'UN FAUNE"   DEBUSSY

PIANOFORTE CONCERTO IN G MINOR   SAINT-SAËNS

    I. Andante sostenuto.
    II. Allegro scherzando.
    III. Presto.

a. MENUET DES FOLLETS
b. BALLET DES SYLPHES   BERLIOZ
c. MARCHE HONGROISE

SOLOIST:
ERNEST HUTCHESON

NOTICE—To subscribers and patrons of The Symphony Concerts

Owing to the number of requests which the management has received, the Board of Directors of the Orchestra Association asks that ladies kindly remove their hats.

The Plum Street Carriage Entrance will be used for the Saturday Evening Concerts. Carriages and Automobiles will not be allowed on Elm Street.

A bugle call will be sounded three minutes before the beginning of each concert.

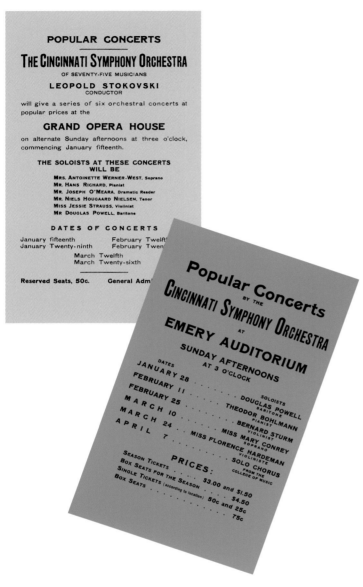

During the 1910-11 season, a series of Popular Concerts was presented at the Grand Opera House. The first CSO "Pops" series began in 1897 at the Hotel Alms as promenade concerts, given to supplement badly needed orchestra income.

In 1889 a bandstand (bottom photo) was built at the Cincinnati Zoological Garden, where afternoon and evening concerts were offered during the summer months. In order to accommodate larger musical groups, a new band shell was built in 1911 and an orchestra of thirty-eight symphony musicians began a fifteen-week summer concert series. The Beaux Arts-style structure was designed by architects Elzner & Anderson with suggestions by CSO conductor Leopold Stokowski.

BEETHOVEN
BACH
HANDEL

3346 · Amusement and Music Stand in the Zoo Park, Cincinnati, O.

If nothing happens will see you Sunday.   Alice   July 1905.

39

The 1911-12 tour took the CSO to Cleveland, St. Louis and Chicago, where the orchestra received unanimous praise from the local critics. Featured on this tour was Stokowski's new bride, Olga Samaroff-Stokowski.

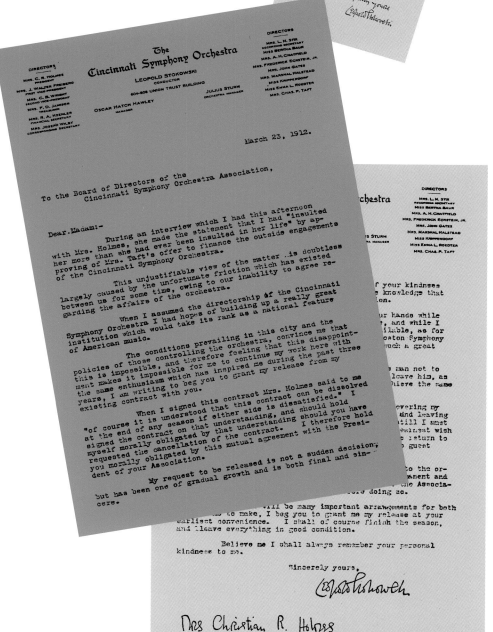

The self-confidence of a young, job-seeking Leopold Stokowski is evident in his letter to Board President Mrs. Christian R. Holmes in 1908. Just three years later bitter feelings between the two led to his resignation.

After a dispute between Board President Mrs. Christian R. Holmes and Mrs. Charles P. Taft, above, Leopold Stokowski's most influential advocate, over the management of the orchestra, an emotional Stokowski suddenly tendered his resignation. Despite pleas for his reconsideration, he was adamant in his request, and on April 13, 1912, he was released from his contract. Two months later, Leopold Stokowski signed a four year contract with the Philadelphia Symphony Orchestra.

44

ERNST KUNWALD

—— 1912 - 1917 ——

Dr. Ernst Kunwald was no stranger to the Cincinnati Symphony Orchestra Board of Directors, having been given serious consideration for the post of music director in 1909. Upon learning of his availability at the conclusion of the Berlin Philharmonic's current season, CSO Board President Mrs. Christian Holmes immediately cabled Kunwald with an offer of a two-year contract at $10,000 per year. He quickly accepted the offer and in May of 1912, Dr. Kunwald and his wife Lina set sail for the United States.

The Queen City and the CSO greeted the Kunwalds in grand style and soon audiences were treated to programs of traditional classical favorites, with an appreciated emphasis on the German fare. The new conductor's thorough understanding of a vast repertory and disciplined approach to rehearsals was welcomed by members of the orchestra, especially after the often over-emotional interpretations of his predecessor. Kunwald, too, appreciated the musical abilities of "his men," comparing them equally with the Berlin Philharmonic.

In 1913, Kunwald, due to his early CSO successes and his acknowledged experience with operatic conducting, was offered an additional contract as Musical Director for the 1914 May Festival. During the next few seasons, the CSO's acclaim under Kunwald's leadership led to an eastern tour with concerts in Boston and New York at Carnegie Hall, as well as a recording contract with the Columbia Phonograph Company. Upon their return, Kunwald and the CSO were wildly greeted by a proud city.

On April 6, 1917, Cincinnatians were stunned by the country's entry into World War I, and the CSO's popular conductor found himself under surveillance as an enemy alien. Although too old to serve in his native Austria's army, Kunwald was resented by many for his loyalty to his homeland. When he became the target of the U.S. Attorney General, Kunwald was interned and eventually deported. The remainder of the 1917-18 symphony subscription concerts were led by five guest conductors.

Ernst Kunwald with the CSO on the stage at Emery Auditorium.

47

ELENA GERHARDT

JULIUS STURM

JOSEF LHEVINNE

EUGENE YSAYE

GERMAINE SCHNITZER

GISELA WEBER

LEOPOLD GODOWSKY

EMIL HEERMANN

CLARENCE WHITEHILL

*The season brochure for 1912-13 featured upcoming guest soloists, including two CSO members,
Emil Heermann and Julius Sturm. Also shown was violinist Eugene Ysaÿe, who would figure
prominently in the orchestra's future.*

CINCINNATI SYMPHONY ORCHESTRA
Personnel - 1912 Program Listing

FIRST VIOLINS
Emil Heermann, *Principal*
Max Schulz
Jean Rietsch
Sandor Kiss
Adolph Borjes
Felix Leipnicker
Raphael Groff
Frank Hancock
Edouard Kopp
George Pierkot
Leo Brand, Jr.
Stanislaw Wrobrewski
Sol. Cohen
Leroy Hancock

SECOND VIOLINS
Carl Wunderle, *Principal*
Hyman Schuler
Edwin Ideler
Carl Burck
Otto Landau
Samuel Shoen
Edwin Memel
Francesco Tallarico
Howard Martin
Tito Ragnetti
Charles Noonan
Porter Manton
Joseph Hayner
John Goodall

VIOLAS
Jacob Tushinsky, *Principal*
Walter Werner
Arthur Brand
Peter Froehlich
Hubert Endres
Max Thal
John Surmann
Jacob Kettenbaum
Richard Donati
Otto Brasch

CELLOS
Julius Sturm, *Principal*
Ignaz Argiewicz
Sigurd Fredericksen
Walter Heermann
Max Froehlich
Armand Baer
James Lauletta
Harry Kaplun

BASSES
Albin Hase
John Zweifel
Gustav Liebholdt
Herman Burck
Gerold Fiore
Frederick Boos
James Tedescki

FLUTES
August Rodemann
Louis Weber
Max Hadricka

PICCOLO
Max Hadricka

FAGOTTS
Gaston Duhamel
Johann Fisnar
Jean Hausknecht

CONTRA FAGOTT
Jean Hausknecht

TROMBONES
Carl Kohlmann
Louis Brand
Carl Eckhardt

OBOES
Albert De Busscher
John Lammers
George Royer

ENGLISH HORN
George Royer

FRENCH HORNS
Gustav Albrecht
Albert Zoellner
Otto Schrickel
Joseph Ringer

TUBA
Peter Bruegmann

PISTON
Joseph Loebker

PERCUSSION
Frank Lohmann
Wm. Bellstedt
Clifford Link

HARP
John Lotito

LIBRARIAN
Leo Brand

ACCOMPANIST
Mrs. Harry J. Plogstedt

Thirty-eight year old cello virtuoso Pablo Casals was a soloist with the CSO in 1915, his first of six appearances in Cincinnati.

THIRD PROGRAM

Friday Afternoon,
November 26. 1915

Saturday Evening,
November 27. 1915

Variations on a Theme by Haydn, Op. 56a........................*Brahms*
    Theme: Chorale Saint Antoni.
    Var. I. Poco piu animato.
       II. Piu vivace.
       III. Con moto.
       IV. Andante con moto.
       V. Vivace.
       VI. Vivace.
       VII. Grazioso.
       VIII. Presto ma non troppo.
       Finale—Andante.

'Cello Concerto........................*Dvorak*
    I. Allegro.
    II. Adagio ma non troppo.
    III. Finale. Allegro moderato.

Symphonic Poem, "Die Toteninsel"........................*Rachmaninoff*
Overture, "Le Corsaire"........................*Berlioz*
    Soloist: PABLO CASALS.

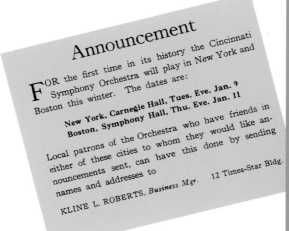

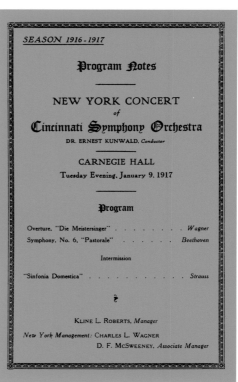

After a highly successful eastern tour, including a concert at Carnegie Hall on January 9, 1917 and final concert in Boston, the orchestra returned to New York for a two-day recording session at the Columbia Phonograph Company. Only two other orchestras, the Chicago Symphony Orchestra and the New York Philharmonic, had recorded before the CSO session. Of the nine selections recorded on the 14th and 15th of January, only four were released.

MOST POPULAR SINGER OF DAY,
CARUSO, TO APPEAR HERE MAY 1

By 1917 the magnificent voice of Enrico Caruso was known to millions through the medium of the phonograph. Caruso had been the leading tenor with the Metropolitan Opera Company for more than a decade and his appearance in Cincinnati, his first ever on a symphonic program, was eagerly awaited. On May 1 an audience of more than 4,000 was treated to a program of three popular arias, after which Caruso was brought back for six encores.

When Enrico CARUSO appears with the Cincinnati Symphony Orchestra in MUSIC HALL, MAY 1st, he will sing "Un Furtiva Lagrima" the subject of the following verse libre—quoted from the New York American.

Ye Towne Gossip
By K. C. B.

Enrico Caruso
NEW YORK City
My dear Caruso
A FEW days ago
I SAID something
IN MY column
ABOUT TENORS.
AND PIMENTO sandwiches
AND BASSOS.
AND MEAT sandwiches
AND I had an idea
AFTER I wrote it
THAT IT was funny
AND SMART.
AND I could imagine people
READING IT
AND Laughing
AND KIDDING the tenors
I CAN imagine anything
AND ANYWAY
I THOUGHT I was smart.
AND SUNDAY night
SOMEBODY TOOK me
TO THE concert
AT THE Metropolitan
AND I had a seat
RIGHT DOWN in the front.
AND YOU came on
BOUNCING ALONG.
ON YOUR TOES
LIKE A ten-year-old kid.
AND YOU smiled
AS THOUGH you meant it
AND STOOD there.
AND WAITED.
TILL YOUR brothers
FROM ACROSS the sea.
CEASED THEIR bravos

AND THE rest of us
CEASED CLAPPING.
AND THEN you sang
AND TOLD us
OF A "Furtive Tear."
AND WHO ever shed it.
I DON'T know
BUT I'M glad she shed it
JUST FOR you.
TO TELL us about it.
AND HOLD us there.
IN ANOTHER world.
THAN THE world outside.
WITH ITS newsboys.
AND THE "three ships sunk."
AND THEN you stopped.
AND I DON'T know
JUST WHAT I did.
BUT THE man who took me.
SAYS I stood up
AND YELLED.
AND MAYBE I did.
AND I don't care
AND YOU sang again
AND THEN again.
AND AFTER a while.
I WENT home.
AND IT'S the next day now.
AND WHAT I said about tenors
THE OTHER day
DOESN'T GO any more.
AND IT WASN'T funny
AND I'M A Smart aleck
AND HALF the time.
I HAVEN'T any idea.
WHAT I'M talking about.
I THANK YOU.

Ernst Kunwald

After the entry of the United States into World War I in 1917, anti-German sentiments were heightened. On the eve of a concert in Pittsburgh on November 22, 1917, after increased pressure by the Daughters of the American Revolution against Austrian Ernst Kunwald's appearance with the CSO, it was decided by city officials that Kunwald would not be allowed to appear. On December 8th he was arrested and held in a federal jail in Dayton, Ohio overnight. On the 10th the CSO Board accepted his resignation, and a month later Ernst Kunwald was re-arrested and interned at Ft. Oglethorpe, Georgia for the remainder of the war.

1917-1918

CINCINNATI SYMPHONY ORCHESTRA

HENRY HADLEY
Guest Conductor

SYMPHONY CONCERTS
TWENTY-THIRD SEASON

TENTH PROGRAM
Feb. 22 - Feb. 23

1917-1918

CINCINNATI SYMPHONY ORCHESTRA

VICTOR HERBERT
Guest Conductor

SYMPHONY CONCERTS
TWENTY-THIRD SEASON

SEVENTH PROGRAM
Jan. 11 - Jan. 12

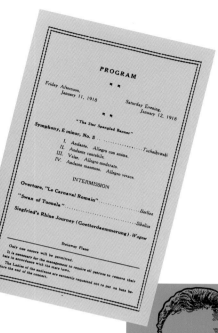

PROGRAM

Friday Afternoon,
January 11, 1918
Saturday Evening,
January 12, 1918

"The Star Spangled Banner"

Symphony, E minor, No. 5 . . . . *Tschaïkowski*

   I. Andante. Allegro con anima.
   II. Andante cantabile.
   III. Valse. Allegro moderato.
   IV. Andante maestoso. Allegro vivace.

INTERMISSION

Overture, "Le Carnaval Romain" . . . . *Berlioz*

"Swan of Tuonela" . . . . *Sibelius*

Siegfried's Rhine Journey (Goetterdaemmerung) . . *Wagner*

Steinway Piano

Only one encore will be permitted.
It is necessary for the management to require all patrons to remove their hats in accordance with the state laws.
The Ladies of the audience are earnestly requested not to put on hats before the end of the concert.

Cincinnati Symphony Orchestra

Edgar Varèse
Guest Conductor

Ninth Popular Concert
Music Hall
Sunday Afternoon
March 17th, 1918

Victor Herbert

After the resignation of Ernst Kunwald, the remaining concerts in the 1917-18 season continued under the direction of five well-received guest conductors. One of them, Eugene Ysaÿe, would become the next CSO music director.

EUGENE YSAŸE

—— 1918 - 1922 ——

When the great Belgian violinist Eugene Ysaÿe opened the 1918-19 season as the new Cincinnati Symphony Orchestra music director and conductor, local audiences needed no introduction to the maestro. During his first American concert tour he had performed in the city with the Cincinnati Orpheus Club on November 22, 1894. Since then, Ysaÿe had appeared with the CSO on five occasions including a performance during the inaugural season in 1895. During the 1917-18 season he had shared conducting duties with other noted musicians after the resignation of Ernst Kunwald.

The sixty-year old virtuoso was a beloved figure throughout the world but found himself a displaced person after the 1914 German occupation of his homeland. In 1918, however, he found a home in Cincinnati, assuming the duties of Music Director of the May Festival. His work with the orchestra and chorus was hailed as a triumph and Ysaÿe was immediately offered the conductorship of the CSO.

Concerts now took on decidedly patriotic themes, playing to the emotions of a country at war, and a sympathetic city held Ysaÿe in great affection. The orchestra flourished under his compassionate, if somewhat undisciplined, leadership, and enthusiasm for the CSO was never higher.

The orchestra's fame was now widespread, with the success of touring engagements throughout the country. But as the number of tours gradually increased over the next few seasons, so did Ysaÿe's discontent, and in 1922 he resigned, at the age of 64 and in poor health, to return to his beloved Belgium.

Eugene Ysaÿe with the CSO at a concert honoring long-time patrons of the orchestra, Mr. and Mrs. Charles P. Taft.

FOURTH LIBERTY LOAN SUBSCRIPTION.
CINCINNATI SYMPHONY ORCHESTRA.
HONOR ROLL.

To the Secretary Of The Treasurer.

The undersigned hereby apply for the number and amount of United States Go
ment Bond of the Fourth Liberty Loan, set opposite their respective names

These are the Liberty loan signatures of the members of the Cincinnati Symphony orchestra.
musicians come from many different lands, but their hearts are all for America. The orchestra
per cent loyal to America and her Allies. Every member of the orchestra, from the distinguished c
tor, Ysaye, to the latest member, subscribed to the fourth Liberty loan. The subscriptions they
through the orchestra amounted to $7,700, but the total amount of their subscriptions, including
made through their home teams, reached $40,000. And the musicians have also subscribed wi
patriotism to the previous loans.

This article appeared in the Times-Star edition of October 24, 1918.

60

CINCINNATI SYMPHONY ORCHESTRA
Personnel - 1920 Program Listing

FIRST VIOLINS
Heermann, Emil, *Concertmaster*
Ysaÿe, Gabriel
Culp, Sigmund
White, Paul
Pack, Ernst
Brand, Leo, Jr.
Memel, Edwin
Knox, Wm.
Silversack, Herbert
Dondero, Arthur
Leipniker, Felix
Henych, Milton
Stojanivitch, S.
Holquin, D.
Berg, H.
Dreyfus, P.
Lawson, R.
Scherzer, B.

SECOND VIOLINS
Poppeldoff, Nico, *Principal*
Schuler, Hyman
Cotton, Walter
Schanes, S.
Groff, J.
Kissane, Donald
Murray, E.
Andrist, Karl
Balendonck, A.
Nisselevitch, N.
Plummer, R.
Eichstadt, J.L.
Morello, C.B.
Jones, L.D.
Tallentyre, W.
Jacky, F.

VIOLAS
Wunderle, Carl
Epstein, David
Burck, Carl
Froehlich, Peter
Weigand, Louis
Kahn, Gordon
Schaufert, Clif N.
Kopp, Wm.
Brasch, Otto

VIOLONCELLOS
Kirksmith, Karl
Heermann, Walter
Vogel, Adolph
Kaster, Jean
Watson, Leonard
Sykora, F.
Mathe, C.
Bowen, A.C.
Angulo, P.

BASSES
Kolmschlag, J.
Berger, Otto
Wathieu, L.
Liebholdt, Gus
Burck, Herman
Whitman, G.B.
Adams, H.J.
Latisch, E.
Kopp, H.
Huston, J.A.

HARP
Vito, J.

FLUTES
Soeller, G.G.
Haun, E.
Hadricka, Max
Weber, Louis

PICCOLO
Hadricka, Max
Weber, L.

OBOES
Rabbu, A.
Chabr, J.
Keleman, F.

ENGLISH HORN
Keleman, F.

CLARINETS
Elliott, J.E.
Gunn, W.
Brand, R.N.

BASS CLARINET
Gunn, W.

BASSOONS
Duhamel, G.
Kennedy, R.
Reines, L.
Jacky, F.

CONTRA BASSOON
Reines, L.

TRUMPETS
Weiss, F.
Schaefer, A.
Heine, Wm.
Kopp, Wm.

HORNS
Albrecht, G.
Ringer, J.
Schrickel, O.
Lind, H.
Kuhn, M.J.

TROMBONE
Alloo, Modeste
Kohlmann, Carl
Wolff, Gus
Berger, O.

TUBA
Huston, J.A.

TYMPANI
Brand, Leo, Sr.

PERCUSSION
Lohman, Frank
Byrnes, H.W.

At Ysaÿe's first concert with the CSO, the program opened with the national anthems of the Allied countries to commemorate the armistice just eleven days prior.

On October 22, 1919 a special concert was given for Belgian King Albert and Queen Elizabeth at Music Hall. Upon their return to Belgium, they recalled that "the best souvenir of our trip is our recollection of Cincinnati's kindness."

PROGRAM

Friday Afternoon,   Saturday Evening,
November 22, 1918   November 23, 1918

The British, Italian, Belgian and French Anthems will be played as
newly orchestrated by Mr. Ysaye.

God Save the King (British Anthem)
Marcia Reale (Italian Anthem)
La Brabançonne (Belgian Anthem)
La Marseillaise (French Anthem)
The Star Spangled Banner

Marche Heroique .... *Saint-Saens*

Concerto, E-flat major, for Violin .... *Mozart*
  I.   Allegro moderato.
  II. Ma poco adagio.
  III. Rondo: Allegretto.

Symphony No. 5, C-minor, op. 67 .... *Beethoven*
  I.   Allegro con brio.
  II. Andante con moto.
  III. Allegro.
  IV. Finale.

INTERMISSION

Paintings .... *Felix Borowski*

"Portrait of a Young Girl."
"The Garden of Night."
"The Festival."
(First Performance in Cincinnati)

a. Chant d'Hiver (second poem for violin
                    and orchestra) .... *E. Ysaye*

b. Introduction and Rondo Capriccioso ...... *Saint-Saens*

Rhapsody, "Espana" .... *Chabrier*

Soloist: JACQUES THIBAUD

Steinway Piano Used

Symphony Concert in honor of the Visit of Their Majesties

KING ALBERT
and
QUEEN ELIZABETH
of
BELGIUM

by the
Cincinnati Symphony Orchestra
Eugène Ysaye ... Conductor

Programme

La Brabançonne (Belgian Anthem).
As orchestrated by Eugène Ysaye

The Star-Spangled Banner.

1. Marche Héroique .... *Camille Saint-Saens*

2. Symphony in D Minor .... *César Franck*
     I.   Lento — Allegro non troppo.
     II. Allegretto.
     III. Allegro non troppo.

3. "Exile," Poem for String Orchestra without Basses ... *Eugène Ysaye*

4. Sylvia Ballet, Suite for Orchestra .... *Léo Delibes*
     I.   Prélude — Les Chasseresses.
     II. Intermezzo — Valse Lente.
     III. Pizzicati.
     IV. Cortège de Bacchus.

61

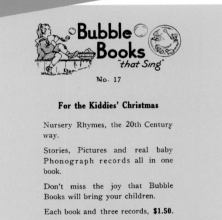
FRIDAY AFTERNOON
PROGRAM

—

Introduction—"The Symphony Orchestra"
MR. THOMAS KELLY

Symphony No. 6, "Surprise," 2nd movement.........*Haydn*

Scherzo from "Midsummer Night's Dream"....*Mendelssohn*

Symphony No. 6, "Pastoral" 1st movement........*Beethoven*

Funeral March of a Marionette ....*Gounod*

Nutcracker Suite ....*Tschaikowsky*
Three Characteristic Dances:
Dance of the Sugar Plum Fairy
Chinese Dance
Dance of the Mirlitons

Ride of the Valkyries......................*Wagner*

*In early 1920, the CSO presented two Young
People's Concerts, the first in the history of the
organization. They were designed to appeal to
ages from eight to fourteen and were narrated
by Thomas J. Kelly, a faculty member at the
Conservatory of Music, with first trombonist,
Modeste Alloo, conducting.*

During Eugene Ysaÿe's tenure as CSO music director, the orchestra toured extensively, including in early 1919, a first-ever trip to several southern cities.

The CSO became the first orchestra to have its music broadcast throughout the country by radio telephone on November 1, 1921, during a concert at the University of Wisconsin.

CINCINNATI ZOOLOGICAL GARDEN

PROGRAM

Sunday, June 26, to Saturday, August 20, 1921

Afternoon Concerts, 2:30 o'clock — Saturday Evening Concert, 8:15 o'clock

Season of Grand Opera and Symphony Concerts

MANAGING DIRECTOR OF OPERA, MR. RALPH LYFORD
CONDUCTOR OF CONCERTS, MR. MODESTE ALLOO

Complete Opera Performances Every Night Except Saturday

Sunday, Aug. 14 and Thursday, Aug. 18..."The Tales of Hoffmann"	Tuesday, Aug. 16..............."Lucia"
Monday, Aug. 15......................................."Faust"	Wednesday, Aug. 17............."Aida"
	Friday, Aug. 19.............."Lohengrin"

SUNDAY, AUGUST 14 and THURSDAY, AUGUST 18, 1921
Evening Program
Conductor, MR. RALPH LYFORD
8:00 P. M.

"THE TALES OF HOFFMANN"
Opera in Prologue and Three Acts by J. Offenbach

CAST

Antonia ....Regina Vicarino	Hermann ....Louis Johnen
Julietta ....Regina Vicarino	Schlemil ....Louis Johnen
Olympia ....Regina Vicarino	Nathanael ....Martha Doerler
Hoffmann ....Salvatore Sciarretti	Luther ....Laurance Wilson
Nicklausse ....Elinor Marlo	Pittichinaccio ....Frank Berling
Dr. Miracle ....Greek Evans	Corps de Ballet
Dappertutto ....Greek Evans	
Coppelius ....Greek Evans	SYNOPSIS OF SCENES
Frantz ....John Niles	Prologue—Luther's Tavern.
Cochenille ....John Niles	ACT I—Crespel's House at Munich. "Antonia."
Spalanzani ....Natale Cervi	ACT II—Venice. A Gallery near the Grand Canal.
Crespel ....Natale Cervi	"Julietta."
A Voice ....Marguerite Bentel	ACT III—The Parlor of Dr. Spalanzani. "Olympia."

MONDAY, AUGUST 15, 1921
Evening Program
Conductor, MR. FRANK WALLER
8:00 P. M.

"FAUST"
Opera in Four Acts and Prologue by Charles Gounod

CAST	SYNOPSIS OF SCENES
	Prologue—Dr. Faust's Laboratory.
Marguerite ....Jean Barondess	ACT I—A Public Square in a German Village.
Faust ....Romeo Boscacci	ACT II—A Garden before Marguerite's Home.
Mephisto ....Italo Picchi	ACT III—The Street before Marguerite's Home.
Valentine ....Mario Valle	ACT IV—The Prison Cell of Marguerite.
Siebel ....Elinor Marlo	
Martha ....Marguerite Bentel	
Wagner ....Louis Johnen	
Corps de Ballet	

TUESDAY, AUGUST 16, 1921
Evening Program
Conductor, MR. RALPH LYFORD
8:00 P. M.

"LUCIA"
Opera in Four Acts by G. Donizetti

CAST

Lucia ....Regina Vicarino
Alice ....Marcella Menge
Edgardo ....Salvatore Sciarretti
Henry Ashton ....Mario Valle
Sir Arthur Bucklaw ......John Niles
Bide-the-Bent ....Italo Picchi
Norman ....Edward Shearer

SYNOPSIS OF SCENES

ACT I—A Park Near the Castle of Lammermoor.
ACT II—An Anti-room in the Castle.
ACT III—The Great Hall of the Castle.
Scene 2—Hall in Lammermoor Castle.
ACT IV—The Cemetery of Ravenswood.

WEDNESDAY, AUGUST 17, 1921
Evening Program
Conductor, MR. FRANK WALLER
8:00 P. M.

"AIDA"
Grand Opera in Four Acts by G. Verdi

CAST

Aida, an Ethiopian Slave..........Jean Barondess
Amneris, Egyptian Princess...Henrietta Wakefield
Rhadames, Captain of the Guard....Romeo Boscacci
Amonasro, King of Ethiopia..........Greek Evans
Ramfis, High Priest................Italo Picchi
The King of Egypt..................Natale Cervi
A Messenger........................John Niles
A Priestess......................Marcella Menge
Grand Corps de Ballet

The plot occurs in Memphis and Thebes, in the epoch of the Pharaohs.

FRIDAY, AUGUST 19, 1921   FINAL PERFORMANCE OF THE SEASON
Evening Program
Conductor, MR. RALPH LYFORD
7:55 P. M.

"LOHENGRIN"
A Romantic Opera in Three Acts by Richard Wagner

The Scene pases in Antwerp. Period, the first half of the tenth century.

CHARACTERS OF THE DRAMA

Lohengrin, a Knight of the Holy Grail......Romeo Boscacci
Henry I, King of Germany................Italo Picchi
Frederick Telramund, a Noble of Brabant....Mario Valle
The Royal Herald......................Natale Cervi
Elsa of Brabant..................Jean Barondess
Ortrud, Wife of Telramund......Henrietta Wakefield
Gottfried, Brother to Elsa..............Gladys Keck

SYNOPSIS OF SCENES

ACT I—A Meadow on the Banks of the Scheldt, near Antwerp.
ACT II—The Citadel of Antwerp.
ACT III—Scene 1—The Bridal Chamber. Scene 2—The Meadow, as in Act 1.

Starr Piano Used

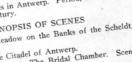
During the summer of 1920, Ralph Lyford, head of the opera department at the Conservatory of Music and CSO Associate Conductor since 1895, presented a seven-week season of light and grand opera at the Cincinnati Zoological Gardens. Several CSO musicians formed the opera orchestra and performed in an enlarged band shell.

Ralph Lyford

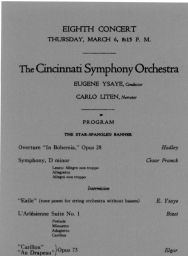

*On this March 6, 1919 concert was
Eugene Ysaÿe's elegy for string
orchestra, "Exile," introduced at the
1918 May Festival. The work
symbolized Ysaÿe's triumph over
tragedy during the war years.*

FRITZ REINER

—— 1922 - 1931 ——

Though only thirty-three years old, Fritz Reiner came to the CSO with impressive credentials, including his most recent accomplishments as conductor of the Dresden Royal Opera since 1914. His arrival in America was reported by an enthusiastic press and once established in Cincinnati, the well-prepared Reiner quickly set about molding the Cincinnati Symphony Orchestra back into a well-disciplined ensemble.

Reiner understood the art of programming. He was determined in his efforts to expand the orchestra's repertoire and mix the familiar with the new. He introduced Ravel to Cincinnati and invited Béla Bártok and Ottorino Respighi to present their compositions in the city.

Under Fritz Reiner the CSO enjoyed great success. Though he was often stern and dictatorial in his approach, he gradually purged the orchestra of its less effective players and the result was a virtuoso symphonic organization, recognized by critics as one of the top five orchestras in the country.

Highly successful Canadian and eastern tours with appearances at Carnegie Hall only served to increase the orchestra's reputation, and while in Washington, D.C., Reiner and the entire orchestra were greeted at the White House by President Calvin Coolidge.

Despite the many triumphs of the CSO during the next few seasons, some influential patrons grew disenchanted with Reiner's frequent absences due to an increasing number of guest-conducting commitments. And when his highly-publicized divorce and romance with actress Carlotta Irwin led to subscription cancellations, the Board decided not to renew his contract.

On April 18, 1931, Fritz Reiner conducted his last concert with the Cincinnati Symphony Orchestra and at the close of the first part of the concert, an appreciative audience and orchestra gave him a ten-minute ovation.

LONGLEY
PHOTO

Russian composer Igor Stravinsky was greeted with wild applause when he conducted a concert of his own works in 1925. He would appear with the CSO two more times.

STRAVINSKY PROGRAM

◻

Friday Afternoon,
March 6, 1925
at 2:30

Saturday Evening,
March 7, 1925
at 8:15

◻

IGOR STRAVINSKY,
Guest Conductor

**Song of the Volga Boatmen, for Wind
Instruments and Percussion**

Scherzo Fantastique, for Orchestra

Suite from "The Fire Bird"
    I (a) Introduction
        (b) L'Oiseau de Feu et sa danse
   II Ronde des Princesses enchantees
  III (a) Danse Infernale du Roi Kastchei
       (b) Berceuse de l'Oiseau de Feu
       (c) Finale

INTERMISSION

Pulcinella

Ballet Suite "Petrouchka"

SEASON 1926-27

ITINERARY

The
Cincinnati Symphony Orchestra

FRITZ REINER, CONDUCTOR
REUBEN LAWSON, MANAGER OF PERSONNEL
LEO BRAND, LIBRARIAN
FERD WEISS, ASSISTANT LIBRARIAN

THURSDAY, NOVEMBER 18
8:30 A. M. (City time) Entire party leaves Cincinnati by special train over
B. & O. R. R. from Fifth and Baymiller Sts., East End car direct
to station. Train will carry diner, two coaches, one Pullman car.
4:00 P. M. Arrive Wheeling.
8:30 P. M. Concert, Court Theatre.

FRIDAY, NOVEMBER 19
9:00 A. M. Leave Wheeling by special train from B. & O. station.
11:30 A. M. Arrive Pittsburgh.
4:00 P. M. Young People's Concert, Syria Mosque.
8:15 P. M. Concert, Syria Mosque.

SATURDAY, NOVEMBER 20
2:15 P. M. Concert, Syria Mosque.

SUNDAY, NOVEMBER 21
7:00 A. M. Leave Pittsburgh by special train on B. & O. R. R. with chair car.
11:00 A. M. Arrive Akron.
3:00 P. M. Concert, Akron Armory.
6:30 P. M. Leave Akron by special train on B. & O. R. R. with chair car.
10:30 P. M. Arrive Pittsburgh.

MONDAY, NOVEMBER 22
2:30 P. M. Rehearsal (with Choir) at Carnegie Hall.
8:15 P. M. Concert, Carnegie Hall.
11:59 P. M. Leave Pittsburgh by special train over B. & O. R. R.

TUESDAY, NOVEMBER 23
9:00 A. M. (City time) Arrive Cincinnati, Baltimore & Ohio station.

INSTRUMENTS—The management of the Orchestra will take all possible care in
handling instruments in transit, but will not be responsible for any damages other
than those for which the railroad or baggage companies can be held directly liable.

HOTELS

Wheeling—Windsor, McClure.
Pittsburgh—Schenley, Webster Hall, Wm. Penn, Ft. Pitt.
Akron—Portage, Bond, Akron.

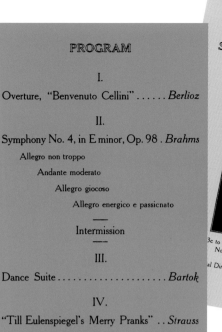

PROGRAM

I.
Overture, "Benvenuto Cellini" . . . . . . *Berlioz*

II.
Symphony No. 4, in E minor, Op. 98 . *Brahms*
Allegro non troppo
Andante moderato
Allegro giocoso
Allegro energico e passionato

—Intermission—

III.
Dance Suite . . . . *Bartok*

IV.
"Till Eulenspiegel's Merry Pranks" . . *Strauss*

CARNEGIE HALL, 57th Street at Seventh Avenue
Wednesday Evening, January 6th, 1926, at 8.30

The
Cincinnati
SYMPHONY ORCHESTRA
FRITZ REINER, Conductor

3c to $2.20
Box seats $2.75 and $2.20
Now on Sale at Carnegie Hall Box Office
Charles Pearson, Manager
al Direction: Concert Management Arthur Judson
(Program on following page)

*The highly successful 1926-27 tour included
concerts in Cleveland, Philadelphia, Pittsburgh,
New York, Washington, D.C. and Toronto.
While in Washington the orchestra visited the
White House, where President Calvin Coolidge
shook hands with each musician.*

ORCHESTRA, WASHINGTON, D. C. FEBRUARY 19, 1927.

CINCINNATI SYMPHONY ORCHESTRA
Personnel - 1922 Program Listing

VIOLINS
Heermann, Emil,
  Concertmaster
Culp, S.
Pack, E.
Brand, L., Jr.
Holguin, D.
Kafka, R.
Knox, W.
Silbersack, H.
Leipnicker, F.
Stojanovitch, S.
Henych, M.
Berg, H.
Phillips, R.
Schoewe, R.
Schuler, H.
Lawson, R.
Cotton, W.
Schanes, S.
Eichstadt, J.
Dondero, A.
Jones, L.D.
Altman, S.
Plummer, R.
Tiemeyer, H.
Neely, U.T.
Jacky, F.
Weiss, F.
Rosenberg, H.

VIOLAS
ten Have, J., *Principal*
Wunderle, C.
Froehlich, P.
Burck, C.
Kahn, G.
Werner, W.
Weigand, L.
Brasch, O.
Zoellner, H.
Schaufert, C.

CELLOS
Kirksmith, K., *Principal*
Heermann, W.
Watson, L.
Angulo, P.
Deak, S.
Kaster, Jean
Bowen, A.
Weis, H.L.
Wolfe, F.A.

BASSES
Kolmschlag, J., *Principal*
Berger, O.
Wathieu, L.
Liebholdt, G.
Burck, H.
Adams, H.J.
Nyberg, Gosta
Latisch, E.
Huston, J.A.

HARP
Vito, J.

FLUTES
Soeller, G.G.
Haun, E.
Weber, L.

PICCOLO
Weber, L.

OBOES
Rabbu, A.
Chabr, J.
Keleman, F.

ENGLISH HORN
Keleman, F.

CLARINETS
Elliott, J.E.
Gunn, W.
Brand, R.N.

BASS CLARINET
Gunn, W.

BASSOONS
Duhamel, G.
Fields, Dall
Reines, L.
Jacky, F.

CONTRA BASSOON
Reines, L.

HORNS
Albrecht, G.
Ringer, J.
Schrickel, O.
Lind, H.
Bellstedt, E.
Hubley, C.

TRUMPETS
Schaefer, A.H.
Kopp, W.J.
Heine, W.
Tiemeyer, H.

TROMBONES
Belgiorni, S.
Kohlman, C.
Swift, A.
Wolff, G.
Berger, O.

TUBA
Huston, J.A.

TYMPANI
Brand, L., Sr.

PERCUSSION
Byrnes, W.
Weiss, F.
Schaufert, C.

LIBRARIAN
Brand, L., Sr.

ORCHESTRA MASTER
Kopp, W.J.

*Right: Concertmaster Emil
Heermann and violinist
Henry Borjes (both standing)
observed as cellist Herbert
Weis marked a score.*

Fritz Reiner

ELEVENTH PROGRAM
❈ ❈

Friday Afternoon,
February 5, 1926

Saturday Evening,
February 6, 1926

❈ ❈

OTTORINO RESPIGHI
Guest Conductor

Concerto in the Mixolydian Mode, for Piano and Orchestra
   I.   Moderato
   II. Lento
   III. Allegro energico (Passacaglia)
OTTORINO RESPIGHI
RALPH LYFORD, Conducting

INTERMISSION

Old Dances and Airs for the Lute (16th and 17th Centuries),
Freely Transcribed for Orchestra by Ottorino Respighi:
(2nd Suite)

   I.   Laura Soave, Balletto con Gagliard, Saltarello
      e Canario (Fabrizio Caroso)
   II. Danza Rustica (Giovanni Battista Besardo)
   III. (a) Campanae Parisienses (Author Unknown)
      (b) Aria (Marin Mersenne)
   IV. Bergamasca (Bernardo Gianoncelli)

Symphonic Poem, "Pini di Roma"

   I.   The Pines of the Villa Borghese
   II. The Pines near a Catacomb
   III. The Pines of the Janiculum
   IV. The Pines of the Appian Way

Steinway Piano Used

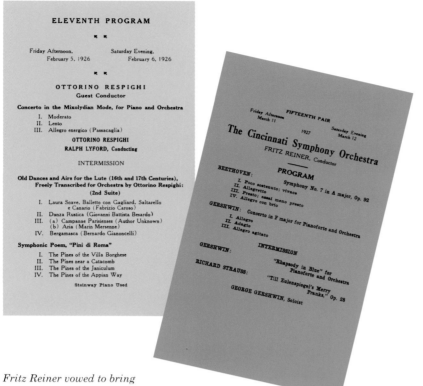

FIFTEENTH PAIR

Friday Afternoon
March 11

1927

Saturday Evening
March 12

The Cincinnati Symphony Orchestra
FRITZ REINER, Conductor

PROGRAM

BEETHOVEN: Symphony No. 7 in A major, Op. 92
    I.   Poco sostenuto; vivace
    II. Allegretto
    III. Presto; assai meno presto
    IV. Allegro con brio

GERSHWIN: Concerto in F major for Pianoforte and Orchestra
    I.   Allegro
    II. Adagio
    III. Allegro agitato

INTERMISSION

GERSHWIN: "Rhapsody in Blue" for
                  Pianoforte and Orchestra

RICHARD STRAUSS: "Till Eulenspiegel's Merry
                  Pranks," Op. 28

GEORGE GERSHWIN, Soloist

Twenty-four year old Polish pianist Vladimir Horowitz electrified Cincinnati audiences with his performance of the Rachmaninoff Concerto No. 3.

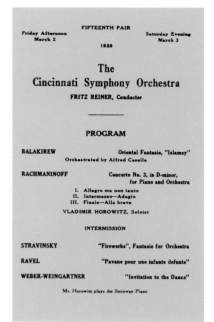

FIFTEENTH PAIR

Friday Afternoon
March 2

1928

Saturday Evening
March 3

The Cincinnati Symphony Orchestra
FRITZ REINER, Conductor

PROGRAM

BALAKIREW   Oriental Fantasie, "Islamey"
Orchestrated by Alfred Casella

RACHMANINOFF   Concerto No. 3, in D-minor,
               for Piano and Orchestra
    I.   Allegro ma non tanto
    II. Intermezzo—Adagio
    III. Finale—Alla breve

VLADIMIR HOROWITZ, Soloist

INTERMISSION

STRAVINSKY   "Fireworks", Fantasie for Orchestra

RAVEL   "Pavane pour une infante defunte"

WEBER-WEINGARTNER   "Invitation to the Dance"

Mr. Horowitz plays the Steinway Piano

Fritz Reiner vowed to bring some modern music to his audiences, and while the richly expressive orchestrations of Ottorino Respighi and jazzy George Gershwin pieces were greeted with enthusiasm, audiences were startled by the works of Béla Bartók.

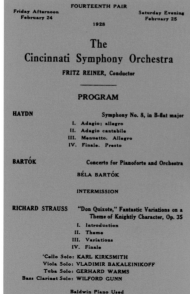

FOURTEENTH PAIR

Friday Afternoon
February 24

1928

Saturday Evening
February 25

The Cincinnati Symphony Orchestra
FRITZ REINER, Conductor

PROGRAM

HAYDN   Symphony No. 8, in B-flat major
    I.   Adagio; allegro
    II. Adagio cantabile
    III. Menuetto. Allegro
    IV. Finale. Presto

BARTÓK   Concerto for Pianoforte and Orchestra
BÉLA BARTÓK

INTERMISSION

RICHARD STRAUSS   "Don Quixote," Fantastic Variations on a
             Theme of Knightly Character, Op. 35
    I.   Introduction
    II. Theme
    III. Variations
    IV. Finale
   'Cello Solo: KARL KIRKSMITH
   Viola Solo: VLADIMIR BAKALEINIKOFF
   Tuba Solo: GERHARD WARMS
Bass Clarinet Solo: WILFORD GUNN

Baldwin Piano Used

Béla Bartók

A CSO rehearsal under Assistant Conductor Vladimir Bakaleinikoff.

These photographs by Paul Briol highlighted various sections of the orchestra.

CINCINNATI
SYMPHONY
ORCHESTRA

This Program Dedicated to

Mr. and Mrs. Charles P. Taft

Season of
1929-1930

EMERY AUDITORIUM
Cincinnati

In 1929 Mr. and Mrs. Charles P. Taft were honored at a pair of concerts under the auspices of the Cincinnati Institute of Fine Arts, which was founded in 1927 to further the arts in Cincinnati.

77

EUGENE GOOSSENS

---- 1931 - 1947 ----

With the hiring of Eugene Goossens as music director and conductor, the CSO Board at long last reunited Cincinnati's two great musical organizations. Goossens' recent success as conductor of the 1931 May Festival gave reassurance to orchestra patrons that the high standards realized by the orchestra to date would continue.

During his career, Goossens gained a reputation as a composer as well as conductor. He had conducted opera at Covent Garden under the tutelage of Sir Thomas Beecham, ballet in London and Europe and symphonic music throughout the world. He came to Cincinnati from Rochester, New York, where he had led the Rochester Philharmonic Orchestra for eight years.

On the podium, Eugene Goossens was polished and refined, admired by many for his mild temperament and quiet authority. He was recognized for his knowledge of British music but demonstrated a flair for conducting contemporary scores. He introduced Cincinnati audiences to Stravinsky's "Le Sacre du Printemps" and championed the work of Shostakovich while presenting a steady fare of Vaughan Williams, William Walton and Benjamin Britten.

During the war years of 1942 and 1943, the CSO premiered several short fanfares commissioned by Goossens from some of the major composers of the day, including Walter Piston, Darius Milhaud, Virgil Thomson, Morton Gould and Howard Hanson. Probably the best known work to come from the project was Aaron Copland's *Fanfare for the Common Man*, still popular at numerous concerts today.

The untiring Goossens continued as director of the May Festival throughout his Cincinnati residence, while adding ballet and grand opera productions to the regular CSO season. At last, however, continued ill-health and a highly attractive offer to head both the Conservatorium and Symphony Orchestra of Sydney, Australia, motivated his resignation in December 1946.

The sixteen-year tenure of Eugene Goossens remains the longest to date.

CINCINNATI SYMPHONY ORCHESTRA
Personnel - 1931 Program Listing

FIRST VIOLINS
Emil Heermann, *Concertmaster*
Howard Colf
Raoul Berger
Leo Brand, Jr.
Stefan A. Sopkin
Samuel Rabinowitz
Ernest Pack
Julian Pulikowski
Adolf Schleue
Anthony Esposito
Henry Borjes
William Morgan Knox
Salo Nagel
Nicholas Gabor
James Werner
Carlo Mastropaolo

SECOND VIOLINS
Alfred Keller
Reuben Lawson
Hyman Schuler
Herbert L. Silbersack
John L. Eichstadt
Felix Leipniker
Hobart Schoch
Samuel Schanes
Walter Shaw Cotton
Fritz Graupner
Harry Berg
Herman Hansen, Jr.

VIOLAS
Vladimir Bakaleinikoff
Herman J. G. Goehlich
August Soendlin
Carl Wunderle
Mikail Stolarevsky
Walter G. Werner
Ernest Lorenz
Rubin Phillips
Georges Vincent Ghilly
Otto Brasch

VIOLONCELLOS
Karl Kirksmith
Walter Heermann
Arthur Zack
Desire Danczowski
Leonard Watson
Arthur C. Bowen, Jr.
Herbert Weis
Arthur L. Knecht
C. K. Findlay
Jean Kaster

BASSES
Lewis Winsel
Joseph Kolmschlag
Alex Trempenau
Alfons Van Reck
Louis R. Cassetta
Gustave Gerhardt
Otto Berger
Gustav Liebholdt

HARPS
Casper Reardon
Joseph Quintile

FLUTES
Ary Van Leeuwen
Louis P. Fritze
Alfred E. Fenboque

PICCOLO
Max Hadrika
Alfred E. Fenboque

OBOES
Marcel J. Dandois
Andre A. Andraud
Arthur D. Gault

ENGLISH HORN
Albert J. Andraud

CLARINETS
Joseph E. Elliott
Wilford Gunn
Richard W. Brand
Herman Hansen, Jr.

BASS CLARINET
Wilford Gunn

BASSOONS
Hans A. R. Meuser
Fred Jacky
Richard Savolini
Leo Reines -

CONTRA BASSOON
Leo Reines

SAXOPHONE
Fred Jacky

HORNS
Max Hess
Gustav Albrecht
Vincent Capasso
Donato Corrado
Hans Lind
Otto Schrickel

TRUMPETS
Henry Wohlgemuth
Louis Davidson
Herbert A. Tiemeyer
Ferd R. Weiss

TROMBONES
Gardell Simons
William B. Wilkins
Carl Kohlmann
Otto Berger

TUBA
William Bell

TYMPANI
Fred W. Noak

PERCUSSION
George J. Carey
Ferd R. Weiss
James J. Rosenberg
Otto Brasch

PIANO
Florence Barbour

LIBRARIAN
Ferd R. Weiss

PERSONNEL MANAGER
Reuben Lawson

MUSIC HALL
ELM STREET
CINCINNATI

FORTY-THIRD SEASON
CINCINNATI SYMPHONY ORCHESTRA
EUGENE GOOSSENS
MUSICAL DIRECTOR

FIRST PAIR SYMPHONY CONCERTS
CONDUCTED BY
EUGENE GOOSSENS

ANALYTICAL NOTES BY
JAMES G. KELLER

FRIDAY AFTERNOON
OCTOBER 16

SATURDAY EVENING
OCTOBER 17

*The Cincinnati Symphony
Orchestra moved back to a
remodeled Music Hall in 1936,
after an absence of 24 years.*

*CSO members leaving Music Hall after
a rehearsal. Seen left to right facing
the camera are: Philip Dreifus; Robert
Cavally; Leo Reines; and Otto Brasch.
On the steps in back are Karl Topie
and Joseph Van Reck.*

85

*A prolific composer,
Eugene Goossens
premiered his
Symphony No. 1 with
the CSO in 1940.*

TWENTIETH PAIR

Friday Afternoon
April 12, 1940
at 2:45 o'clock

Saturday Evening
April 13, 1940
at 8:30 o'clock

PROGRAM

EUGENE GOOSSENS, Musical Director

MENDELSSOHN .... Overture, Fingal's Cave, Op. 26

GOOSSENS .... Symphony, Op. 58
"To My Colleagues of the Cincinnati Symphony Orchestra"
(World Premiere)

I   Andante; allegro con anima
II Andante espressivo, ma con moto
III Divertimento. Allegro vivo
IV Finale. Moderato; alla breve

INTERMISSION

BRAHMS .... Symphony No. 1 in C-minor, Op. 68

I   Un poco sostenuto; allegro poco sostenuto
II Andante sostenuto
III Un poco allegretto e grazioso
IV Adagio; più andante; allegro non troppo ma con brio

The Baldwin is the official piano of the Cincinnati Symphony Orchestra

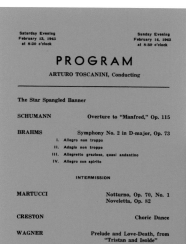

Saturday Evening
February 13, 1943
at 8:20 o'clock

Sunday Evening
February 14, 1943
at 8:30 o'clock

PROGRAM

ARTURO TOSCANINI, Conducting

The Star Spangled Banner

SCHUMANN   Overture to "Manfred," Op. 115

BRAHMS   Symphony No. 2 in D-major, Op. 73
I. Allegro non troppo
II. Adagio non troppo
III. Allegretto grazioso, quasi andantino
IV. Allegro con spirito

INTERMISSION

MARTUCCI   Notturno, Op. 70, No. 1
Noveletta, Op. 82

CRESTON   Choric Dance

WAGNER   Prelude and Love-Death, from
"Tristan and Isolde"

As an additional number, Mr. Toscanini
will conclude the program with the
Overture to "The Mastersingers," by Wagner

Famed conductor Arturo Toscanini's appearance in Cincinnati during the 1942-43 season marked his first in the United States away from the eastern seaboard. The seventy-six year old maestro was then conductor of the NBC Symphony Orchestra, well known for its dynamic radio broadcast concerts.

Arturo Toscanini

A Half Century of Golden Music
1894-95   1944-45
GOLDEN JUBILEE YEAR
The Story of the Cincinnati Symphony Orchestra

The Jubilee Competition
To stimulate and foster creative talent

William Grant Still
Composer of the prize overture

Music is the creation of man — the ability to create music, a divine gift, but, a gift that must be fostered and encouraged so that potential great music is not lost to the world.

The Cincinnati Symphony Orchestra is deeply aware of its responsibility to encourage modern composers. That it sincerely believes in this responsibility is shown by the frequent appearances on its programs of the works of these young moderns.

This year, the Cincinnati Orchestra carried such sponsorship one step further. It announced a nationwide competition, with a prize of a $1000.00 War Bond, for a Jubilee Overture to commemorate the Golden Anniversary Season. The committee of three elected to judge the entries were prominent figures in the world of music—Eugene Goossens, Deems Taylor, noted music commentator, composer and critic, and Pierre Monteux, Conductor of the San Francisco Symphony Orchestra.

From the 39 entries that poured in, the judges were unanimous in their choice of a composition by William Grant Still of Los Angeles.

Mr. Still, one of the country's most promising modern composers, is a native Mississippian, has African, Indian and white blood in his veins. He has made a special study of Negro spirituals, which he believes are the most important native American contribution to music. His most famous composition, Afro-American Symphony, has been widely played in both Europe and America; his opera, "Troubled Land," was performed this past February under the direction of Leopold Stokowski.

The prize-winning composition, "A Festive Overture," which was written and scored in the space of a few weeks, has a definite American flavor. It bespeaks the pride of the composer in his native land, the warmth of the American people, the grandeur of scenic America.

That the overture is a valuable addition to American music is eloquent proof of the competition's intrinsic worth and the fulfillment of its purpose—to stimulate and foster creative talent.

ELEVENTH PAIR

Friday Afternoon
January 19, 1945
at 2:15 o'clock

Saturday Evening
January 20, 1945
at 8:30 o'clock

PROGRAM

EUGENE GOOSSENS, Musical Director

JUBILEE PROGRAM
(January, 1895—January, 1945)

THE STAR SPANGLED BANNER

UNITED NATIONS NATIONAL ANTHEM, No. 11—
NEW ZEALAND

STILL, WM. GRANT   Festive Overture
World Premier of Prize-winning Overture (Cincinnati
Symphony Jubilee Competition)

RAVEL   Introduction and Allegro for Harp,
Flute, Clarinet and Strings
Harp Solo, VOJMIR ATTL

STRAWINSKY   Symphonic Poem for Orchestra—
"The Song of the Nightingale"

WAGNER   March of Homage

INTERMISSION

TCHAIKOVSKY   "Manfred" Symphony in B-minor, Op. 58
I. Lento Lugubre (The Mental Anguish of Manfred)
II. Vivace con spirito (By the Waterfall)
III. Andante con moto (Pastorale)
IV. Allegro con fuoco (Subterranean Palace of
Arimanes and Death of Manfred)

The CSO celebrated its 50th anniversary during the 1944-45 season. As part of the Golden Jubilee celebration, a nationwide competition was held for a Jubilee Overture. The winning entry, out of 37 total, was a work by William Grant Still. The Mississippi native won a first prize thousand dollar war bond for his "Festive Overture."

o the right, sits the cello choir, the most versatile of the strings of the orchestra. To the left are seen some of the wood-winds and the brasses.

Emil Heermann, the concertmaster (left), leads the first violin choir through the intricate melodies of a Brahms symphony.

EUGENE GOOSSENS, Musical Director of the Cincinnati Symphony Orchestra, returns from a triumphal tour, as guest conductor of some of England's greatest orchestras, to take his familiar place on the podium at Music Hall at the December 2-3 Symphony Concerts.

The harps, the most attractive of the orchestral instruments, add to the beauty of the percussion section.

The Candid Camera Catches The Symphony Orchestra At Rehearsal In Music Hall.

—Enquirer Photos by Al Kuprion.

e bassoon has a al personality. metimes it is the ilosopher of the or-estra — sometimes the clown.

A portion of the bass choir, often called the foundation of a symphony orchestra.

The percussion section provides many music effects for the orchestra with its tympani, drums, phones, cymbals, bells, triangles, etc.

he violas play melodies of istinctive character and pro-

The second violin choir takes

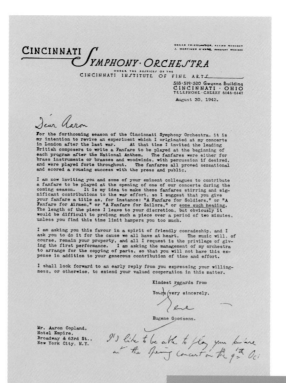

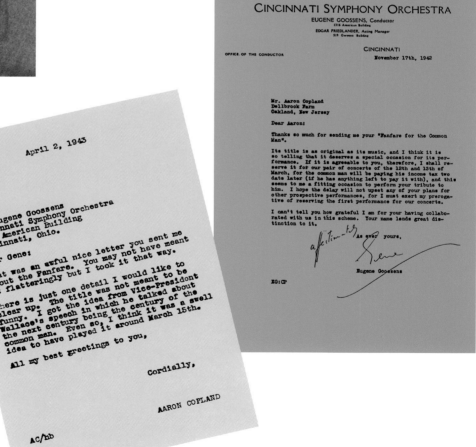

Aaron Copland's widely-known "Fanfare for the Common Man" was commissioned by CSO Music Director Eugene Goossens in 1942 as part of a request by Goossens of several recognized composers of the time to submit musical contributions to the war effort. Other fanfares submitted included: Walter Piston's "Fanfare for the Fighting French," Morton Gould's "Fanfare for Freedom," and Howard Hanson's "Fanfare for the Signal Corps."

Have a Coke

DRINK
Coca-Cola

STRAWS

Quaker
ENRICHED
Farina
NET WT. 14 OZ.
NEW!
CREAMY SMOOTH
WHEAT CEREAL

BUILD WITH BLOCKS   BUILT
FUN FOR EVERYONE   REAL
BLOCK
CITY
Model Homes, Stores, Garages,
Buildings, Churches.
THE MOST AUTH
PLASTIC BLOCK

Original HAL-SAM HEWN
AMERICAN
LOGS
REPRODUCE IN MINIATURE DETAILED SCALE THE
HIGH-CUT, SQUARE—TIMBERS OF PIONEER DAYS
by
Halsam
SENIOR
SIZE
3/4"
LOGS

REMOVE BOTTLE
BEFORE INSERTING
NEXT NICKEL

WHEN COIN STORE

Coca-Cola

PETER
and
WOLF
RUDOLPH
The Red-Nosed Reindeer
45
Golden
45
RPM

RAIL
CROSSING
ROAD

STOP
ON
SIGNAL

ROCKETS

LIONEL   SP
6257

REGULAR GRIND
SANKA
COFFEE
97%
CAFFEIN
Lets You Sleep

Tom Thumb
CASH REGISTER

1803 OHIO 1953
SESQUI-CENTENNIAL

THOR JOHNSON

——— 1947 - 1958 ———

American born and trained, Thor Johnson became the seventh CSO music director in 1947, having served as conductor of the Symphony Orchestra of the Juilliard School of Music the previous year.

During his college years at the University of North Carolina and the University of Michigan, Johnson gained experience directing various university and civic orchestras and choral groups. Due to a sense of responsibility to perform contemporary works, he presented, during his career, some 120 premieres, half of which he commissioned himself, and half given by the CSO under his baton.

His eleven-year tenure as head of the CSO saw the introduction of Neighborhood Family Concerts as well as an increase in Young People's and Junior High concerts, thereby widening the degree of exposure for the orchestra in the community. Johnson became a highly respected and popular figure.

Thor Johnson was accorded many honors while director of the CSO, including six honorary degrees, international recognition as co-conductor of the Symphony of the Air on its extensive tour of the Orient in 1955, and his appointment by President Eisenhower to the ten-man Advisory Committee on the Arts.

At the end of the 1957-58 season, Thor Johnson resigned to accept a post as head of the Orchestral Department at Northwestern University School of Music.

CSO violist Siegfried "Sigi" Mozart Humphreys showed the lighter side of classical music in these caricatures of his fellow CSO musicians, which appeared in the Sunday, October 26, 1947 issue of the Cincinnati Enquirer.

Above: The first concert of the 1947-48 season, at which Thor Johnson conducted Beethoven's "Eroica" as one of his first numbers, suggested to Humphreys the new conductor's artistic position – on top of the world.

Right: Fred W. Noak had no real tiff with Shostakovitch, but he nearly tore his tympani to tatters when it came to the Russian's Fifth Symphony – under Leonard Bernstein's baton.

Below: The haste with which orchestra members packed, unpacked and dressed on tour occasioned several contretemps like this – an exchange of coats between two trumpeteers, Herbert Tiemeyer (6 feet 5) and Michael Devonchek (5 feet 6). They never appeared on stage this way.

CINCINNATI SYMPHONY ORCHESTRA
Personnel - 1947 Program Listing

FIRST VIOLINS
Sigmund Effron, *Concertmaster*
Emil Heermann
Philip Dreifus
Carlo Mastropaolo
Hobart Schoch
William M. Knox
John Beroset
Ernest Pack
Henry Borjes
Leo Brand
Reuben Segal
Adolf Schleue
James Werner
Salo Nagel
Jean Ten Have
Raymond Costello

SECOND VIOLINS
Herbert Silbersack
Hyman Schuler
Samuel Schanes
Nicholas Gabor
Arthur Dondero
Milton Henych
Charles Charkins
Fritz Graupner
Peter Rhalyis
Reuben Lawson
Henry Shaw
Carl Rubinoff

VIOLAS
Eric Kahlson
Joseph Sherman
Herman J. Goehlich
August Soendlin
Harry Berg
Peter Froehlich
Siegfried M. Humphreys
Rubin Phillips
Ernest Lorenz
Mary J. Leeds

VIOLONCELLOS
Walter Heermann
Fritz Bruch
Leonard Watson
Arthur Bowen
Herbert Weis
Arthur Knecht
Karl Topie
Victor Rice
Fritz Manczyk
John C. Harnish

DOUBLE BASSES
Louis Winsel
Joseph Van Reck
Harold Roberts
Gustave Gerhardt
Charles Medcalf
Andrew Wolf
Richard Topper
Otto Berger

HARP
Anna Bukay

FLUTES
Alfred E. Fenboque
Robert Cavally

PICCOLO
Ruth Duning

OBOES
Marcel J. Dandois
Andre A. Andraud

ENGLISH HORN
Albert J. Andraud

CLARINETS
Emil Schmachtenberg
Eugene Frey

BASS CLARINET
Fred Schuett

BASSOONS
Hans A. R. Meuser
Dorothy Dickinson

CONTRA BASSOON
Leo Reines

FRENCH HORNS
James L. Pierce
Verne B. Reynolds
Mathias J. Kuhn
Hilbert Mosher
Vincent Capasso

TRUMPETS
Henry Wohlgemuth
Herbert A. Tiemeyer
Michael Denovchek

TROMBONES
Adolph D'Ambrosio
Ernest Glover
William B. Wilkins

TUBA
Samuel Green

TYMPANI
Fred W. Noak

PERCUSSION
Otto Brasch
Harold J. Thompson
George J. Carey

Thor Johnson conducting the
Orchestra at Music Hall during the
60th anniversary season.

*Three ladies, hats and all, at the Arts &
Handicraft Exhibit in 1948.*

*The first Symphony Ball was held in 1954 to
benefit the symphony. It was planned by the
Women's Committee and held at the Cincinnati
Art Museum.*

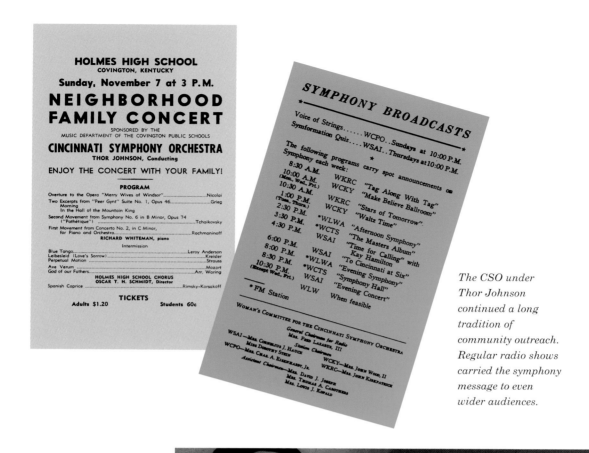

The CSO under Thor Johnson continued a long tradition of community outreach. Regular radio shows carried the symphony message to even wider audiences.

Thor Johnson (center), flanked by then-CSO manger Craig Hutchinson and concertmaster Sigmund Effron as they admired the 1952-53 season brochure.

The highlight of the 1954-55 season was the American premiere of Jean Sibelius' musical interpretation of Shakespeare's "The Tempest." The production was directed by Basil Langton, seen in this photograph standing center in the top balcony, in association with the Antioch College Arena Stage. Noted Shakespeare scholar Arthur Lithgow, center stage, was cast in the role of Stephano. The orchestra, on stage in full view of the audience and wearing sailor berets, was directed by Thor Johnson.

The
CINCINNATI SYMPHONY ORCHESTRA
THOR JOHNSON, MUSIC DIRECTOR
proudly presents
The United States Orchestral Premiere of
SHAKESPEARE'S
THE TEMPEST

with
music by
JAN SIBELIUS

performed
in honor of
the composer's
89th birthday
December 8

Full Dramatic Production
with
ANTIOCH AREA THEATRE
assisted by
CINCINNATI MUSIC-DRAMA GUILD
MUSIC HALL
DECEMBER 3 at 2:15 P.M. — DECEMBER 4 at 8:30 P.M.

One of Thor Johnson's sixty commissioned works featured four musical views of Cincinnati. The work was premiered in 1953 in honor of Ohio's Sesquicentennial celebration.

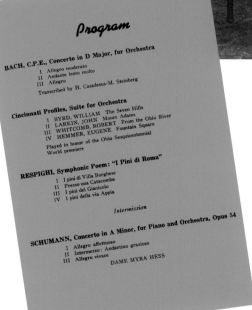

Program

BACH, C.P.E., Concerto in D Major, for Orchestra
I   Allegro moderato
II Andante lento molto
III Allegro
Transcribed by H. Casadesus–M. Steinberg

Cincinnati Profiles, Suite for Orchestra
I   BYRD, WILLIAM The Seven Hills
II LARKIN, JOHN Mount Adams
III WHITCOMB, ROBERT From the Ohio River
IV HEMMER, EUGENE Fountain Square
Played in honor of the Ohio Sesquicentennial
World premiere

RESPIGHI, Symphonic Poem: "I Pini di Roma"
I   I pini di Villa Borghese
II Presso una Catacomba
III I pini del Gianicolo
IV I pini della via Appia

Intermission

SCHUMANN, Concerto in A Minor, for Piano and Orchestra, Opus 54
I   Allegro affettuoso
II Intermezzo: Andantino grazioso
III Allegro vivace   DAME MYRA HESS

GET READY FOR SOME FUN!

The riotous
Concert Comedienne
and Vocal Satirist . . .

ANNA
RUSSELL

Guest Artist
at the opening

POP CONCERT

SUNDAY, NOVEMBER 23 AT 3:00 P.M.
MUSIC HALL

CINCINNATI SYMPHONY ORCHESTRA
THOR JOHNSON, Conducting

MAX RUDOLF

——— 1958 - 1969 ———

Before he turned twenty, Max Rudolf knew he would become a conductor. After his early music studies, the Frankfort-am-Main, Germany native secured a leading position in the Darmstadt Opera House at age twenty-five. In the early 1930s, his appearances as a symphonic conductor with the Berlin Philharmonic drew enthusiastic press reviews "...a born musical leader...a great success."

When the political situation in central Europe became difficult in 1935, Rudolf fled to Switzerland, and in 1940 he and his family were granted an immigration visa to the United States. In New York, Rudolf joined the staff of the Metropolitan Opera in 1945. When Rudolf Bing took over in 1950, Rudolf was appointed artistic administrator. His extensive guest conducting experience while at the Met offered him exposure throughout the country and in 1958, Rudolf was offered the position of Music Director of the Cincinnati Symphony Orchestra.

Max Rudolf's tenure with the CSO saw many changes, including increases in personnel and concerts; Kinderkonzerts and In-School concerts for children and an exclusive long-term contract with Decca Records.

The highlight of the Rudolf years was the selection of the orchestra by the U.S. Department of State Office of Cultural Presentation for a ten-week world tour, the first world tour by an American symphony orchestra under government sponsorship.

Max Rudolf's gregarious personality endeared him to many Cincinnatians and his accomplishments while CSO music director led to his appointment as Music Director Emeritus.

The CSO under Max Rudolf in concert at the Herod Atticus Amphitheater in Athens, Greece during the first leg of the 1966 historic world tour.

1960: A youngster peered into the bell of Sam Green's tuba with assistance from his friend, who also managed to mug for the camera.

Double bassist Harold Roberts demonstrated what surely must have seemed like a towering instrument to these delighted children attending a "Kinderkonzert."

KINDERKONZERT

A holiday special for children by
Cincinnati Symphony Orchestra
CARMON DELEONE, conductor

Peter and
the Wolf

Narrated by WCPO-TV Star
NICK CLOONEY

Danced by
Bobby Ziegler   Lettie Coyle
Gary Golsch   Linda Hils
Nancy Ziegler   Vicki Schmidt
Shirley Eilers   Debbie Tranter
Kathy Huenefeld   Bonnie Ziegler
                             ALSO

Children lined up to buy their "Kinderkonzert" tickets at the Baldwin store on 4th Street in 1961.

Arts patrons J. Ralph Corbett and Patricia Corbett are pictured here in Hong Kong in 1966 during the CSO's around-the-world tour. The Corbetts and The Corbett Foundation have been loyal and consistent supporters of the CSO, especially in many of the orchestra's milestones. Among the Corbett's numerous generous gifts to the CSO have been support for the 1969 European tour; the J. Ralph Corbett Pavilion at Riverbend; a $1 million challenge grant to the Orchestra's 1993 deficit elimination campaign; and major support for the restoration of, and continuing improvements to, Music Hall which directly benefit the Orchestra. In addition, The Corbett Foundation has provided leadership gifts to many deserving projects throughout the Cincinnati arts and education community.

J. Ralph Corbett served on the Board of Trustees of the CSO from 1960 until his death in 1988 including terms as Chairman of the Board and Trustee Emeritus. Patricia Corbett is currently a Trustee Emeritus and has served on the Board since 1984.

CINCINNATI SYMPHONY ORCHESTRA
Personnel - 1958 Program Listing

FIRST VIOLINS
Sigmund Effron, *Concertmaster*
Henry Borjes
Hobart Schoch, *Librarian*
Leo Brand
William Knox
John Beroset
Salo Nagel
Ernest Pack
Raymond Costello
Reuben Segal
Achille Di Russo
Vladimir Lukashuk
Ronald Konieczka
Arnold Schatz
Karl Payne
William Miller
Siegfried Humphreys

SECOND VIOLINS
Herbert Silbersack, *Principal*
Henry Shaw
Stephen Elsaesser
Connie Kiradjieff
Milton Henych
Charles Charkins
John Swales
Fritz Graupner
Donald Gibson
Adolph Schleue
Patricia Conway
Reuben Lawson
 Personnel Manager

VIOLAS
Eric Kahlson, *Principal*
Joseph Sherman
Herman Goehlich
Rubin Phillips
Harry Berg
Anthony Esposito
Theodore Wadl
Peter Froehlich
Virginia Di Russo
Ernest Lorenz

VIOLONCELLOS
Arthur Bowen, *Principal*
Arthur Knecht
Victor Rice
Herbert Weiss
Karl Topie
Leonard Watson
Fritz Manczyk
Marian Beers
Elizabeth Wilber
Charles Findlay

DOUBLE BASSES
Harold Roberts, *Principal*
Joseph Van Reck
Gustave Gerhardt
Charles Medcalf
Richard Topper
Andrew Wolf
Robert Bradley
Gen Parchman

HARP
Anna Bukay

FLUTES
Alfred Fenboque, *Principal*
Robert Cavally

PICCOLO
Jack Wellbaum

OBOES
Dennis Larson, *Principal*
Andre Andraud

ENGLISH HORN
Ferdinand Prior

CLARINETS
Emil Schmachtenberg, *Principal*
Keith Harman

BASS CLARINET
Frederick Schuett

BASSOONS
Hans Meuser, *Principal*
George Campbell

CONTRA BASSOON
Leo Reines

FRENCH HORNS
James Pierce, *Principal*
Charles Tarlton
Mathias Kuhn
Alfred Myers
Vincent Capasso

TRUMPETS
Eugene Blee, *Principal*
Michael Denovchek
Herbert Tiemeyer

TROMBONES
Tony Chipurn, *Principal*
Ernest Glover
Betty Glover

TUBA
Samuel Green

TYMPANI
Jennings Saumenig

PERCUSSION
Glenn Robinson, *Principal*
Trudy Drummond

PIANO
Babette Effron

Max Rudolf with oboist Dennis Larson and flutist Alfred Fenboque in 1958.

Max Rudolf was fond of spotlighting CSO musicians as soloists, a tradition which continues through the present life of the Orchestra. Pictured in a publicity photo for the "CSO Artists" concert in January 1964 were Erik Kahlson, violist, who was soloist in Berlioz's "Harold In Italy"; and wind players George Hambrecht, flute; Dennis Larson, oboe; Richard Waller, clarinet; Otto Eifert, bassoon; and Michael Hatfield, French horn. The quintet performed Etler's Concerto for Wind Quintet and Orchestra.

The Symphony Jazz Quintet's early seeds were sown during the Orchestra's historic world tour in 1966, when a group of versatile CSO musicians jammed with local jazzers in clubs along the tour route. By 1967 the group was firmly established with (above, left to right) David Frerichs, drums; Marie Speziale, trumpet; Frank Proto, piano; Paul Piller, trombone; and Robert Bradley, double bass.

109

From the World Tour program:
"On August 2, 1966, the Cincinnati Symphony Orchestra embarked on an around-the-world tour under the auspices of the Cultural Presentations Program of the United States Department of State. During the subsequent 68 days, the Orchestra performed 42 concerts in 15 nations, traveled a distance of over 33,000 miles and became the first American professional orchestra to circle the globe.

The company consisted of 120 persons, including a full-time physician and several orchestra member's wives.

A specially chartered plane transported the Orchestra's ten tons of equipment – a load which included a new Baldwin SD-10 concert grand piano and more than 500 pounds of music."

Maestro Max Rudolf and Associate Conductor Erich Kunzel performed the conducting duties and pianist Lorin Hollander accompanied the Orchestra as guest soloist.

The itinerary included the countries of Greece, Turkey, Lebanon, Israel, Yugoslavia, Switzerland, India, Malaysia, Singapore, Hong Kong, Philippines, Republic of China, Japan and Korea.

CSO members board an airport bus in the rain prior to departing for New York City and a concert at Carnegie Hall. From left: Babette (Mrs. Sigmund) Effron, CSO pianist; Concertmaster Sigmund Effron; Gen Parchman, bass; Ernest Glover, trombone;, and Herbert Silbersack, violin.

Members of the Cincinnati Symphony Club made some interesting musical decorations for the annual bazaar in 1965. These women were fashionably dressed, with hats and gloves still the norm.

The Symphony of Fashion was always a successful fundraiser for the Orchestra.

112

The popular Eight O'Clock series was an innovation in 1962. The first concert on November 13th of that year was designed around the theme, "From Foreign Lands and People...A Musical Journey Abroad," and included "Finlandia," Mendelssohn's "Italian" Symphony and "The Moldau," among others.

Volunteers put in long hours during season ticket phonathons.

Lifetime supporters of much that makes Cincinnati one of America's most liveable cities, Louise and Louis Nippert have generously and quietly given their financial support and their expertise to many of Cincinnati's arts institutions. Pictured here in 1963 at a Cincinnati Opera Association performance – for which the CSO is the official orchestra – the Nipperts presented opportunities unique to Cincinnati when, as owners of the Cincinnati Reds and supporters of the CSO, they created financial and promotional bridges between these two Cincinnati major league "teams."

HELP

An Exhibition Documenting
The Endangered
Cincinnati Union Terminal.

It is Being Presented
As Part of a Bigger Effort
to Preserve the
Building and its Murals.

January 11 thru February 5
12 to 5 Sun
10 to 5 Tues thru Sat

Contemporary Arts Center
115 E. Fifth Street
Cincinnati, Ohio 45202

CINCINNATI REDS
WORLD CHAMPS '75

BACH JONATHAN LIVINGST

SHAUN CASSIDY

DONNY & MARIE · NEW

OLIVIA NEWTON-JOHN
FROM THE MOTION PICTURE
GREASE

STEVIE WONDER
THE BEST OF THE GUESS WHO

Cincinnati
Symphony
Orchestra
Thomas Schippers
Eighty-Sixth Season

THOMAS SCHIPPERS
—— 1970 - 1977 ——

Charisma could have been a word invented to describe Thomas Schippers. Barely 40 years old when he arrived in Cincinnati, the tall, handsome conductor had enjoyed a star-quality career.

After early studies at Philadelphia's Curtis Institute of Music and Yale University, the teenage Schippers was encouraged by his piano teacher, Olga Samaroff, wife of former CSO music director Leopold Stokowski, to audit a conducting class at Tanglewood. Barely two years later, in 1950, he conducted the New York premiere of Gian Carlo Menotti's first full-length opera "The Consul." Still in his twenties, Schippers next conducted the premiere of Aaron Copland's "The Tender Land," and the first televised performance of Menotti's soon-to-be Christmas classic, "Amahl and the Night Visitors."

Following came engagements with the New York Philharmonic, alternating with Leonard Bernstein on the podium during a trip to the Soviet Union. Then came debuts at the La Scala Opera House and the 1964 Bayreuth Festival, premieres in Milan and several appearances with the Metropolitan Opera for the busy maestro.

In 1969 at the peak of his career, Schippers was regarded as the likely successor to Bernstein for the post of music director of the New York Philharmonic. But the job went to Pierre Boulez and New York's loss was Cincinnati's gain when, in 1970, Schippers was named music director of the Cincinnati Symphony Orchestra.

The Queen City quickly fell under the charm of Thomas Schippers, as he became a very visible personality in the community. But fortune turned against him in 1973 when his wife Nonie died after a long struggle with cancer. Just four years later, Schippers himself was diagnosed as having lung cancer, and in December 1977, the 47 year-old maestro was gone.

Cincinnati
Symphony
Orchestra
Thomas Schippers MUSIC DIRECTOR
Seventy-Sixth Season

Thomas Schipper's musical intensity was captured in this rehearsal photograph.

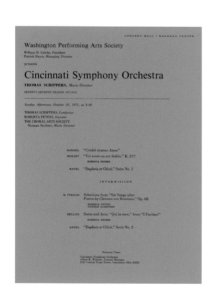

In 1971, the CSO was presented in concert at the Kennedy Center in Washington, D.C. Former CSO general manager Albert K. Webster, along with Washington Performing Arts Society managing director Patrick Hayes, admired the large "three-sheet" outside the hall.

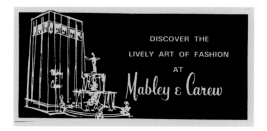

In 1971, Erich Kunzel was on the podium and Van Cliburn was soloist for one of the CSO's Riverfront Stadium appearances. Other notables who appeared with the CSO at Riverfront were Al Hirt, Benny Goodman and Roberta Flack. At one memorable stadium concert, booming cannons on the field broke the glass in the stadium boxes.

In February 1972, the Women's Committee sponsored a gala called "In A Festive Garden." In the "Conductor's Corner" were Thomas Schippers at the piano; Erich Kunzel on double bass; and Carmon DeLeone, drums. At the time, Kunzel was resident conductor and DeLeone was assistant conductor under music director Schippers.

CSO cheerleaders excited the crowd at this outdoor event.

Max Rudolf founded the Cincinnati Youth Orchestra (now known as the Cincinnati Symphony Youth Orchestra) in 1964. Longtime CSO concertmaster Sigmund Effron, the youth orchestra's first conductor, led the group for seven years with the conviction that youngsters should "have an opportunity to play in a symphonic group which devotes itself to the works of the great masters." The present CSYO is made up of 96 high school musicians from 31 area schools.

August 1974: Erich Kunzel and the CSO on an unusual stage—a barge on the Ohio River at Fernbank Park.

A little girl holds the symbol of the Saturday morning concerts initiated in the 1970s. Still popular today, the "Lollipop" concerts reach out to Greater Cincinnati's large family population. The budding French hornist on the right shows promise as a future CSO member.

The city of Cincinnati and the nation's music community were saddened by the news of the death of CSO conductor laureate, Thomas Schippers. Even though Schippers had been ill for some time, citizens were shocked that the charismatic Schippers' all-to-brief tenure in Cincinnati was over.

Thomas Schippers Is Dead at 47; Conductor of Opera, Symphony

Thomas Schippers

Mark Troffel

By DONAL HENAHAN

Thomas Schippers, conductor laureate of the Cincinnati Symphony Orchestra and one of the foremost of young American conductors, died in New York City Friday night of lung cancer.

Mr. Schippers, who was 47 years old, had been ill for some time, forcing him to cancel a number of recent concerts.

Fortune gave Thomas Schippers everything, then brutally snatched it away. The musician from Kalamazoo, Mich., 6 feet 3 inches tall and handsome as a Hollywood leading man, rose quickly to become one of the golden boys of his generation of American conductors. He himself could hardly believe it. "Unbelievable luck and an incredible series of accidents are the only explanations for all of it," he once told an interviewer.

And talent, of course. The critics acknowledged he had plenty of that. His

of the Lemonade Opera's singers went to audition for Mr. Menotti, who was then casting his first full-length opera, "The Consul," and Mr. Schippers went along to play the piano for her. Mr. Menotti was more impressed with the pianist than with the singer, and hired him to coach the singers for "The Consul."

Luck once again tapped Mr. Schippers on the shoulder when shortly before the opera's New York premiere, in 1950, the regular conductor fell ill and the young conductor was asked to take his place. "If that isn't luck, what is?" Mr. Schippers later remarked.

After conducting for three months in New York, Mr. Schippers was sent to Europe by Mr. Menotti to record the score for a film of "The Medium." After service in the Army, with a tour of duty in Germany, he returned to the United

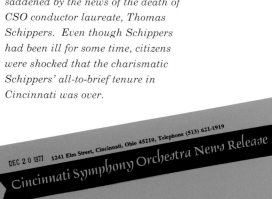

DEC 20 1977   1241 Elm Street, Cincinnati, Ohio 45210, Telephone (513) 621-1919

Cincinnati Symphony Orchestra News Release

for immediate release:

THOMAS SCHIPPERS DEAD AT 47

Thomas Schippers, Music Director of the Cincinnati Symphony Orchestra since 1970 and its Conductor Laureate since November of this year, died at his New York City residence this evening of lung cancer. He was 47.

One of the most eagerly sought-after conductors in the world in both the symphonic and operatic fields, the Michigan-born maestro was widely recognized for his musical brilliance, electric stage presence, handsome looks, and glamourous lifestyle.

Born March 9, 1930 in Kalamazoo, he ear[...] early in life and enjoyed a nearly 30-year [...] in Europe and the United States. Accepting [...] age of 40 with the Cincinnati Symphony--he [...] tra's 83-year history and conducted his f[...] tember 1970--he had made his conducting [...] of New York, shortly after having recei[...] young conductors' contest. Two years [...] Menotti's Pulitzer-prize-winning oper[...] premiere of the composer's "Amahl and [...]

Appointed to the conducting sta[...] Mr. Schippers at the age of 25 made [...] with the New York Philharmonic, and [...] ond youngest ever to direct at the [...] At the Met, he held the record of [...] opening night of the Met's new ho[...] Samuel Barber's "Antony and Cleo[...]

After the untimely death of Thomas Schippers, the
highly-respected Walter Susskind served as CSO
Music Advisor from 1978 to 1980. His vast
conducting experience included engagements with the
Concertgebouw of Amsterdam, the Philadelphia
Orchestra, the London Philharmonic and the
Cleveland Orchestra, to name just a few. While in
Cincinnati, Walter Susskind led the CSO during the
Orchestra's 85th anniversary season, as well as a 17-
day tour of Florida and the east coast, concluding
with a concert at Carnegie Hall.

An elaborate birthday cake was grandly
displayed in the foyer of Music Hall
on the occasion of the CSO's 85th
anniversary in 1979.

MICHAEL GIELEN

—— 1980 - 1986 ——

German-born Michael Gielen received his early musical training in Buenos-Aires after his family fled the Nazis. In Argentina he studied with fellow refugees Furtwängler, Böhm and Kleiber. The young Gielen seemed destined for the stage, with an actor father and actress mother.

During his career his conducting experience has covered most of Europe, various American orchestras, major music festivals and guest appearances from South America to Australia. He was chief conductor of the Stockholm Opera, music director of the Belgian State National Orchestra and *Generalmusikdirektor* of the Frankfurt Opera.

After some early suspicions over Gielen's rumored "ultra-modernist" approach to programming, the maestro and audiences warmed to each other and he premiered and recorded several acclaimed works with the Cincinnati Symphony Orchestra.

While in Cincinnati, Gielen continued his work in Europe as Artistic Director of the Frankfurt Opera. He assumed the post of Chief-Conductor of the Southwest German Radio Orchestra after leaving the CSO in 1986.

For his many accomplishments both in Cincinnati and abroad, Michael Gielen was awarded the Prize for Culture from the state of Hesse, Federal Republic of Germany and the Post-Corbett Award in the Performing Arts category for his outstanding contribution to the arts in Cincinnati.

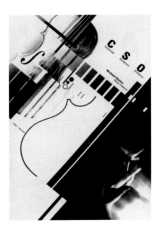

Michael Gielen, CSO Music Director from 1980-86, was warmly welcomed at this reception in September 1980.

CINCINNATI SYMPHONY ORCHESTRA
Personnel - 1980 Program Listing

FIRST VIOLINS
Phillip Ruder, *Concertmaster*
  Anna Sinton Taft Chair
Andrew Zaplatynsky, *Associate Concertmaster*
Rebecca Green, *Associate Concertmaster*
Conny Kiradjieff
Larrie Howard
Sylvia Samis
Borivoje Angelich
John Beroset
James Braid
Raymond Castello
Joseph Fafard
Donald Gibson
Ronald Konieczka
Gayna Mandelbaum
Lois Reid
Darla Da Deppo Riley
Oscar Francis Rubens
Stephen Schaefer

SECOND VIOLINS
Rosemary Waller
  Al Levinson Chair
*Henry Shaw
DeAnne Cleghorn
David Moore
Margaret Wasserman
Yvonne Bizet
Mary Ruth Bryant
Harold Byers
Denise Doolan
Morris Edley
Siegfried Humphreys
Vladimir Lukashuk
Keylor Noland
Serge Shababian
Ronald Shapey
John Swales

VIOLAS
Marna Street
  Louise D. & Louis Nippert Chair
*Raymond Stilwell
Ronald Arron
Mark Cleghorn
Sari Eringer
Paul Frankenfeld
Robert Howes
Allen Martin
Mary Olson
Joseph Somogyi
Grigori Tarakansky

VIOLONCELLI
Peter Wiley
  Irene & John J. Emery Chair
*Geraldine Sutyak
Dana Rusinak
Norman Johns
Fritz Manczyk
Susan Marshall
Laura McLellan
Elizabeth Silkwood
Charles Snavely
Carlos Zavala

BASSES
Barry Green
*Charles Medcalf
Richard Topper
Ronald Bozicevich
Robert Bradley
Frank Proto
Charles Van Ornum
Andrew Wolf

HARPS
Anna Bukay
Linda Wellbaum

FLUTES
George Hambrecht
  Charles Friederich Goss Chair
Rochelle Doepke
*Kyril Magg

PICCOLO
Jack Wellbaum

OBOES
Richard Johnson
Michael Kenyon
*Dennis Larson

ENGLISH HORN
William Harrod

CLARINETS
Richard Waller
Carmine Campione
*Richard Porotsky

BASS CLARINET
Thomas LeGrand

BASSOONS
Otto Eifert
Martin James
Frank Heintz

CONTRABASSOON
Ernst Dieter van der Bent

FRENCH HORNS
Michael Hatfield
*Milton Blalack
Robert Schauer
Alfred Myers
Charles Tarlton

TRUMPETS
Philip Collins
Eugene Blee
Steve Pride
*Marie Speziale

TROMBONES
Tony Chipurn
James Eastman
Betty Glover

TUBA
Michael Thornton

TIMPANI
Eugene Espino

PERCUSSION
William Platt
Edward Wuebold
Richard Jensen

HARPSICHORD
Eiji Hashimoto

PIANO & CELESTA
Rotating position
  James P. Thornton Chair

PERSONNEL MANAGERS
Jack Wellbaum
Richard Topper, *Assistant*

LIBRARIANS
Marshall Burlingame
Mary Judge, *Assistant*

STAGE MANAGERS
Joseph D. Hopper
Thomas J. Thoman

*Assistant or Associate

Former principal cellist Peter Wiley was soloist for a gymnasium concert in Batesville, Indiana in 1980. The CSO still includes Batesville on its regional tours; weather permitting, the concert is held outdoors.

Erich Kunzel leads the Cincinnati Symphony Orchestra in the opening of its annual free series on Fountain Square in 1982.

Riverbend Gala Grand Opening

Inaugural Season 1984	Wednesday, July 4 8:00 p.m.	Cincinnati POPS Orchestra	Erich Kunzel Conductor

Erich Kunzel
conducting

Ella Fitzgerald
guest artist

Neil Armstrong
special guest

Frank Proto	The Riverbend Festival Fanfare *World Premiere*
Francis Scott Key	The National Anthem

Opening Night Dedication Ceremony

Aaron Copland	*Lincoln Portrait*, for Speaker and Orchestra

Neil Armstrong

Cole Porter	"From This Moment On" from *Out of This World*
Duke Ellington	"Satin Doll"
Arr. Nelson Riddle	Lerner and Loewe Medley
Brooks/Waller/Razaf	"Ain't Misbehavin'"
Richard Rodgers	"Mountain Greenery" from *Garrick Gaieties*
Porter	"It's All Right With Me" from *Can-Can*

Ella Fitzgerald

Intermission

George Gershwin	"'S Wonderful" from *Funny Face*
Arr. James Jones	Duke Ellington Medley
Porter	"Let's Do It" from *Paris*
	"Blue Moon" from *Hollywood Party*
Rodgers	"People" from *Funny Girl*
Jule Styne	St. Louis Blues
W.C. Handy	

Ella Fitzgerald

Piotr Ilyich Tchaikovsky	1812 Overture

This concert is being broadcast live by public radio stations throughout the United States. It is being produced by WGUC-FM 90.9, Cincinnati, for American Public Radio.

The Cincinnati POPS Orchestra sign is a gift from the late Mrs. Jules J. Fern.
The Riverbend Festival Intermission Fanfare was written by Frank Proto.
The Baldwin is the official piano of the Cincinnati POPS Orchestra and Riverbend Music Center.
The Cincinnati POPS Orchestra records for the Moss Music Group and Caedmon.
Cincinnati POPS Orchestra blazers are by Palm Beach Incorporated.

The July 4, 1984 opening concert at Riverbend Music Center, the stunning amphitheater designed by architect Michael Graves and owned by the CSO, and the outdoor summer home of the CSO and Pops, drew a capacity crowd. Officially named the Hulbert Taft, Jr. Center for the Performing Arts, J. Ralph Corbett Pavilion in honor of its major donors, Riverbend is nationally recognized as an important venue not only for the CSO and Pops concerts, but for acts ranging from middle-of-the-road, to country, to rock, to alternative music.

The CSO's "Concerts in the Park" have drawn enthusiastic audiences since their inception in 1967. Pictured below is a crowd in Covington's Devou Park.

Michael Gielen championed the music of twentieth-century composers such as Lutoslawski, Zemlinsky, and Schoenberg, and introduced a number of important compositions to Cincinnati audiences.

C S O

Michael Gielen and the Cincinnati Symphony Orchestra carry this program to New York City's Carnegie Hall on March 14.

Friday,
March 4,
11:00 a.m.

Saturday,
March 5,
8:30 p.m.

George Crumb

Variazioni

Michael Gielen
conducting

All-orchestral
program

Introduzione: Lento; Tema:
Andante semplice
Pezzo antifonale: Allegretto grazioso
Toccata: Feroce, violente
Notturno (Fantasia I): Lentamente
e misterioso
Scherzo: Molto vivace, Trio estatico:
Andante tranquillo; Burlesca:
Molto vivace
Cadenza (Fantasia II): Molto adagio –
Ostinato: Allegro drammatico –
Elegia (Fantasia III): Lento desolato;
Tema: Poco adagio

Anton Bruckner

Symphony Number 5 in B-flat Major
Adagio, Allegro; Adagio; Allegro
Adagio
Scherzo: Molto vivace
Adagio; Allegro moderato

*First performances at these concerts.

wguc FM 90.9 PRESENTS

The

**CINCINNATI SYMPHONY
ORCHESTRA**

Recorded concerts from the 1980-1981 Season

Sunday evenings at 8:00 p.m.

Hosted by Gary Barton

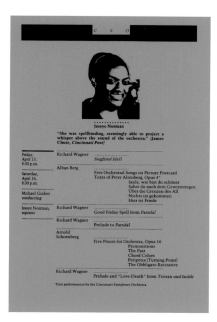

Jessye Norman

"She was spellbinding, seemingly able to project a whisper above the sound of the orchestra." (James Chute, *Cincinnati Post*)

Friday, April 15, 8:30 p.m.	Richard Wagner	*Siegfried Idyll*
Saturday, April 16, 8:30 p.m.	Alban Berg	Five Orchestral Songs on Picture Postcard Texts of Peter Altenberg, Opus 4*
		Seele, wie bist du schöner
Michael Gielen conducting		Sahst du nach dem Gewitterregen Über die Grenzen des All
		Nichts ist gekommen
Jessye Norman, soprano		Hier ist Friede
	Richard Wagner	Good Friday Spell from *Parsifal*
	Richard Wagner	Prelude to *Parsifal*
	Arnold Schoenberg	Five Pieces for Orchestra, Opus 16
		Premonitions
		The Past
		Chord Colors
		Peripetia [Turning Point]
		The Obbligato Recitative
	Richard Wagner	Prelude and "Love-Death" from *Tristan und Isolde*

*First performances by the Cincinnati Symphony Orchestra.

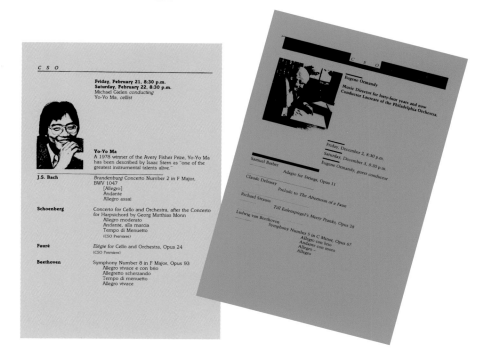

Friday, February 21, 8:30 p.m.
Saturday, February 22, 8:30 p.m.
Michael Gielen *conducting*
Yo-Yo Ma, *cellist*

Yo-Yo Ma
A 1978 winner of the Avery Fisher Prize, Yo-Yo Ma has been described by Isaac Stern as "one of the greatest instrumental talents alive."

J.S. Bach	Brandenburg Concerto Number 2 in F Major, BWV 1047
	[Allegro]
	Andante
	Allegro assai
Schoenberg	Concerto for Cello and Orchestra, after the Concerto for Harpsichord by Georg Matthias Monn
	Allegro moderato
	Andante, alla marcia
	Tempo di Menuetto
	(CSO Premiere)
Fauré	*Elégie* for Cello and Orchestra, Opus 24
	(CSO Premiere)
Beethoven	Symphony Number 8 in F Major, Opus 93
	Allegro vivace e con brio
	Allegretto scherzando
	Tempo di menuetto
	Allegro vivace

Eugene Ormandy
Music Director for forty-four years and now Conductor Laureate of the Philadelphia Orchestra.

Friday, December 2, 8:30 p.m.
Saturday, December 3, 8:30 p.m.
Eugene Ormandy, *guest conductor*

Samuel Barber	Adagio for Strings, Opus 11
Claude Debussy	Prelude to *The Afternoon of a Faun*
Richard Strauss	*Till Eulenspiegel's Merry Pranks*, Opus 28
Ludwig van Beethoven	Symphony Number 5 in C Minor, Opus 67
	Allegro con brio
	Andante con moto
	Allegro
	Allegro

Throughout its long history, the CSO has continued to present the outstanding artists of the day to its audiences. Each season the best soloists and conductors, young and old, appear with the CSO in Cincinnati and on tour.

Shortly after joining the CSO in 1966, double bassist Frank Proto began his second career as arranger and composer. Many of his large orchestral pieces, including those commissioned by CSO bassist Barry Green and former CSO conductors Thomas Schippers and Michael Gielen, have been premiered by the Cincinnati Symphony Orchestra.

Proto has also written a number of works for the Cincinnati Pops Orchestra, including his now-classic, "Casey at the Bat," recorded by the Pops under Erich Kunzel and narrator Johnny Bench, former Cincinnati Reds Hall of Fame catcher.

Frank Proto's compositions also include chamber works and music in the jazz idiom. His latest commission from the CSO will be performed during the centennial season.

JESÚS LÓPEZ-COBOS
—— 1986 - PRESENT ——

Maestro Jesús López-Cobos is currently in his ninth season as Music Director of the Cincinnati Symphony Orchestra, after his appointment as the eleventh CSO music director in 1986.

While a student at the University of Granada in his native Spain, López-Cobos began conducting the university choir with no formal training. But his talent was obvious and after studies in Italy and Vienna, he made his European debut in 1969 at the Prague Festival and operatic debut that same year in Venice.

Jesús López-Cobos soon became a celebrated opera and orchestral conductor in Europe and America, his impressive list of appointments including general music director of the Deutsche Oper Berlin, principal guest conductor of the London Philharmonic and music director of the Spanish National Orchestra. His prestigious assignments have won him recognition throughout the world as one of today's foremost conductors.

During his tenure in Cincinnati, the personable maestro has led the CSO to international acclaim. In the fall of 1990, Jesús López-Cobos and the orchestra embarked on a highly successful tour of the Far East, during which they performed for capacity audiences in Taiwan and throughout Japan. Their five-city tour of the West Coast during the 1991-92 season was the first in the orchestra's history.

As CSO Music Director for the Centennial Celebration season, Jesús López-Cobos continues the long tradition of bringing the finest music to the Cincinnati community.

CINCINNATI SYMPHONY ORCHESTRA
Personnel - 1986 Program Listing

FIRST VIOLINS
Phillip Ruder, *Concertmaster*
  Anna Sinton Taft Chair
Rebecca Culnan, *Associate Concertmaster*
Sylvia Samis, *Assistant Concertmaster*
Conny Kiradjieff
Larrie Howard
Michelle Edgar
†Borivoje Angelich
Gayna Mandelbaum Bassin
James Braid
Raymond Castello
Mimi Dennison
Joseph Fafard
Donald Gibson
Lois Reid Johnson
Ronald Konieczka
Darla Da Deppo Riley
Oscar Francis Rubens
Stephen Schaefer

SECOND VIOLINS
Rosemary Waller
  Al Levinson Chair
*Henry Shaw
Catherine Lange
DeAnne Cleghorn
David Moore
†Harold Byers
Drake Crittenden
Denise Doolan
Morris Edley
Rebecca Kruger
Vladimir Lukashuk
Sylvia Mitchell
Paul Patterson
Serge Shababian
Ronald Shapey
John Swales

VIOLAS
Marna Street Ramsey
  Louise D. & Louis Nippert Chair
*Paul Frankenfeld
†Mark Cleghorn
Robert Howes
Allen Martin
Judith Martin
Mary Olson
Steven Rosen
Joseph Somogyi
Raymond Stilwell
Sari Eringer Thoman

CELLOS
**Geraldine Sutyak
  Irene & John J. Emery Chair
Dana Rusinak
†Daniel Culnan
Norman Johns
Laura McLellan
Susan Marshall-Petersen
Charles Snavely
Carlos Zavala

BASSES
Barry Green
Richard Topper
†Ronald Bozicevich
Wayne Anderson
Frank Proto
Charles Van Ornum
Rick Vizachero

HARPS
Caitriona Yeats
Linda Wellbaum

FLUTES
George Hambrecht
  Charles Friederich Goss Chair
Rochelle Doepke
*Kyril Magg

PICCOLO
Jack Wellbaum

OBOES
Richard Johnson
  Josephine I. & David J. Joseph, Jr. Chair
Michael Kenyon
*Lon Bussell

ENGLISH HORN
William Harrod

The CSO in rehearsal under Maestro López-Cobos.

CLARINETS
Richard Waller
Carmine Campione
*Richard Porotsky

BASS CLARINET
Ronald Aufmann

BASSOONS
Otto Eifert
Martin James
Frank Heintz

CONTRABASSOON
Ernst Dieter van der Bent

FRENCH HORNS
Robin Graham
Charles Bell
Robert Schauer
Milton Blalack
Charles Tarlton

TRUMPETS
Philip Collins
Eugene Blee
Steve Pride
*Marie Speziale

TROMBONES
Tony Chipurn
James Eastman
Peter Norton

TUBA
Michael Thornton

TIMPANI
Eugene Espino

PERCUSSION
William Platt
Edward Wuebold
Richard Jensen

PIANO & CELESTA
Rotating Position
  James P. Thornton Chair

PERSONNEL MANAGERS
Jack Wellbaum
Richard Topper, *Assistant*

LIBRARIANS
Mary Judge-Vila
Richard Evert, *Assistant*

STAGE MANAGERS
Joseph D. Hopper
Thomas J. Thoman

†Begins the alphabetical listing
of players who participate in a system of
rotated seating within the string section.
*Assistant or Associate Principal
**Acting Principal

The CSO Chamber Players series, initiated in 1988, presents the musicians of the CSO in an intimate chamber music setting – historic Memorial Hall, a beautifully restored Beaux Arts building designed by Samuel Hannaford and located next to Music Hall. The series features music chosen, performed and even sometimes written by the CSO musicians themselves. Jesús López-Cobos made a rare appearance with the Chamber Players in May 1991, conducting a chamber ensemble in music by Vivaldi.

To date Maestro Jesús López-Cobos and the Cincinnati Symphony Orchestra have made twelve recordings for Telarc, beginning with a 1987 release of music by Manuel de Falla that was named a "Record of the Year" by Stereo Review magazine.

145

In the fall of 1990, the Cincinnati Symphony Orchestra and the
Cincinnati Pops Orchestra embarked on a tour of the Far East, their
first international tour in more than a quarter of a century.   A total
of 112 musicians, 12 staff members, three stage hands and family,
friends and supporters traveled to 11 cities in Japan and Taiwan.
The CSO under Jesús López-Cobos and Assistant Conductor Keith
Lockhart and the Pops Orchestra under Erich Kunzel performed a
total of 19 concerts during the 30-day trip.

During their whirlwind tour, the group had a chance to visit several historic sites, participate in a prestigious telecast, and experience the excitement of the coronation of a new emperor. And for 21 musicians who were with the orchestra in Japan on the 1966 world tour, it was a chance to renew old acquaintances.

147

Popular concerts have been a cornerstone of the Cincinnati Symphony Orchestra's existence almost from the Orchestra's inception. Announcements for popular concerts appeared in CSO program books in 1896, though the actual program books have not been located. Beginning with Leopold Stokowski's tenure, light classics and popular music of the day were regularly presented to ever-increasing audiences by the musicians of the Cincinnati Symphony Orchestra.

Erich Kunzel's first conducting appearance in Cincinnati, in October 1965, was a sold-out Eight O'Clock Pops concert at Music Hall. When the CSO Board of Trustees officially established the Cincinnati Pops Orchestra in 1977, Erich Kunzel was named the orchestra's Conductor. Dubbed "The Prince of Pops" by The Chicago Tribune, Maestro Kunzel has led the Cincinnati Pops to unprecedented successes at home, on tour and through its numerous recordings (46 to date with Telarc International, see page 160), forty of which have appeared on "Billboard" magazine's charts of best-selling albums. The Cincinnati Pops' famous theme concerts include "Chiller," a Halloween spectacular for which orchestra, conductor and audience dress in costume (shown below). "Billboard" listed in its November 1994 100th Anniversary issue the all-time 40 leaders on its Classical Crossover chart. Five Cincinnati Pops recordings are designated on this list, including the "Chiller" album.

The Cincinnati Pops' Telarc recordings have earned four Grammy Award nominations: for "Lincoln Portrait and Other Works," "A Disney Spectacular," "The Music Man," and "Amen!" "American Jubilee" won the prestigious Grand Prix du Disque in 1989, and "A Disney Spectacular" was also named Classical Record of the Year in Japan that same year. Erich Kunzel is the most successful "Billboard" Classical Crossover recording artist in history, earning that category's Artist of the Year award for an unprecedented four consecutive years. Maestro Kunzel was also awarded the 1989 Sony Tiffany Walkman Award in recognition of his "visionary recording activities." To top it all off, recordings by Erich Kunzel and the Cincinnati Pops have sold over 5 million copies!

A word about "Billboard": Founded in November 1894 in Cincinnati by William H. Donaldson and James H. Hennegan, its original intent was devotion to "the interests of advertisers, poster printers, bill posters, advertising agents and secretaries of fairs." It gradually took on the entertainment world as well, and by 1909 was known as "The Billboard – America's Leading Amusement Weekly."

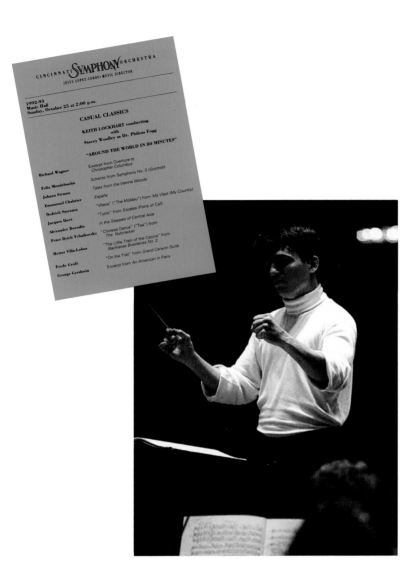

After having joined the CSO as Assistant Conductor in August of 1990, Keith Lockhart is currently the Associate Conductor of both the Cincinnati Symphony Orchestra and the Cincinnati Pops Orchestra. His duties include designing and conducting all of the CSO's Young People's concerts, the Lollipop Family Concerts and the Riverbend Family Concert.

In addition to subscription concerts with the CSO and CPO, Lockhart has received acclaim for appearances with the Chicago Symphony Orchestra, the Los Angeles Philharmonic and the Boston Pops, where he has returned for several engagements.

The 1994-95 season will be the third for Keith Lockhart as Music Director of the Cincinnati Chamber Orchestra and the fourth season for the CSO's popular Casual Classics, an informal classical series of his own design.

The 1994-95 Centennial Season is the sixth for Ivan Fischer as Principal Guest Conductor of the Cincinnati Symphony Orchestra. The native Hungarian launched his international career in 1976 when he won the Rupert Foundation Conducting Competition. In the early 1980s, he conducted the London Symphony Orchestra on tours of Britain and the Far East.

From 1984 to 1989, Maestro Fischer was Music Director of the Kent Opera and also conducted major productions throughout Europe. His North American appearances include concerts with the symphony orchestras of Chicago, Houston, Los Angeles, Pittsburgh and many others.

In 1983, Ivan Fischer founded the Budapest Festival Orchestra with his friend, the noted pianist Zoltan Kocsis. The highly acclaimed orchestra has performed at some of the world's most prestigious music festivals and its recordings of the works of fellow Hungarian Béla Bartók have won major awards.

CINCINNATI SYMPHONY ORCHESTRA

1994-95 Centennial Season

Jesús López-Cobos, Music Director
Max Rudolf, Honorary Music Director
Erich Kunzel, Cincinnati Pops Conductor
Ivan Fischer, Principal Guest Conductor
Keith Lockhart, Associate Conductor

First Violins
Rebecca Culnan, *Acting Concertmaster*
 Anna Sinton Taft Chair
Sylvia Samis, *Acting Associate Concertmaster*
Conny Kiradjieff
Larrie Howard
Michelle Edgar Dugan
†Gayna Mandelbaum Bassin
Darla Da Deppo Bertolone
James Braid
Joseph Fafard
Oscar Rubens Fernandez
Donald Gibson
Gerald Itzkoff
Lois Reid Johnson
Ronald Konieczka
Rebecca Kruger
Sylvia Mitchell

Second Violins
°Catherine Lange
 Al Levinson Chair
§Scott Mozlin
‡Hye-Sun Park
David Moore
†Borivoje Angelich
Drake C. Ash
Harold Byers
Chiun-Teng Cheng
DeAnne Cleghorn
Denise Doolan
Paul Patterson
Stephen Schaefer
Serge Shababian
Stacey Woolley

Violas
Marna Street, *Principal*
 Louise D. & Louis Nippert Chair
*Paul Frankenfeld
**Julian Wilkison
†Mark Cleghorn
Robert Howes
Allen Martin
Judith Martin
Mary Olson
Steven Rosen
Joseph Somogyi
Raymond Stilwell
Sari Eringer-Thoman

Cellos
Eric Kim, *Principal*
 Irene & John J. Emery Chair
*Daniel Culnan
 Ona Hixson Dater Chair
**Dana Rusinak
†Norman Johns
Matthew Lad
Laura McLellan
Susan Marshall-Petersen
Charles Snavely
Geraldine Sutyak
Carlos Zavala

Basses
Barry Green, *Principal*
*James Lambert
**Matthew Zory, Jr.
†Wayne Anderson
Ronald Bozicevich
Frank Proto
Charles Van Ornum
Rick Vizachero

Harp
°Juliet Stratton

Flutes
Randolph Bowman, *Principal*
 Charles Friederich Goss Chair
Rochelle Doepke
*Kyril Magg

Piccolo
Joan Voorhees

Oboes
Richard Johnson, *Principal*
 Josephine I. & David J. Joseph, Jr. Chair
Michael Kenyon
*Lon Bussell

English Horn
William Harrod

Clarinets
Richard Hawley, *Principal*
 Emma Margaret & Irving D. Goldman Chair
Carmine Campione
*Richard Porotsky

Bass Clarinet
Ronald Aufmann

Bassoons
William Winstead, *Principal*
Hugh Michie
*Martin James

Contrabassoon
Frank Heintz

French Horns
Robin Graham, *Principal*
 Mary M. & Charles F. Yeiser Chair
*Thomas Sherwood
**Duane Dugger
Robert Schauer
Milton Blalack
Charles Bell

Trumpets
Philip Collins, *Principal*
Steven Pride
Douglas Lindsay
*Marie Speziale

Trombones
Tony Chipurn, *Principal*
James Eastman

Bass Trombone
Peter Norton

Tuba
Michael Thornton, *Principal*

Timpani
Eugene Espino, *Principal*
 Matthew & Peg Woodside Chair

Percussion
William Platt, *Principal*
Richard Jensen
David Fishlock

Keyboards
Michael Chertock
Rotating Position
 James P. Thornton Chair

Personnel Manager
Rosemary Waller

Librarians
Mary Judge
Sandra Pearson, *Assistant*

Music Assistant for the Pops
Crafton Beck

Conducting Assistant
Carol Nies

Stage Managers
Joseph D. Hopper
Thomas J. Thoman

†Begins the alphabetical listing of
 players who participate in a system
 of rotated seating within the string
 section.

* Associate Principal
**Assistant Principal
° Acting Principal
§ Acting Associate Principal
‡ Acting Assistant Principal

D I S C O G R A P H Y

CINCINNATI SYMPHONY ORCHESTRA COMMERCIAL RECORDINGS 1917 - 1994

OFFENBACH: Tales of Hoffmann: Barcarolle. Ernst Kunwald, conductor. Columbia. 1917.

STRAUSS, JOHANN II: On the Beautiful Blue Danube. Ernst Kunwald, conductor. Columbia. 1917.

DELIBES: Coppélia: Waltz of the Hours. Ernst Kunwald, conductor. Columbia. 1917.

HALVORSEN: Triumphal Entry of the Bojaren. Ernst Kunwald, conductor. Columbia. 1917.

MASSENET: Le Cid: Navarraise. Eugene Ysaÿe, conductor. Columbia. 1920.

RUBENSTEIN: Monastery Bells. Eugene Ysaÿe, conductor. Columbia. 1921.

RIMSKY-KORSAKOV: Scheherazade, first movement. Eugene Ysaÿe, conductor. Columbia. 1921.

MAILLART: Les dragons de Villars. Eugene Ysaÿe, conductor. Columbia. 1921.

LASSEN: Festival Overture. Eugene Ysaÿe, conductor. Columbia. 1921.

MENDELSSOHN: A Midsummer Night's Dream: Scherzo. Eugene Ysaÿe, conductor. Columbia. 1921.

DELIBES: Naila valse: Intermezzo. Eugene Ysaÿe, conductor. Columbia. 1921.

OFFENBACH: Orpheus in Hades: Overture. Eugene Ysaÿe, conductor. Columbia. 1920.

RIMSKY-KORSAKOV: Scheherazade, third movement. Eugene Ysaÿe, conductor. Columbia. 1921.

MACBETH: Love in Idleness. Eugene Ysaÿe, conductor. Columbia. 1921.

CZIBULKA: Hearts and Flowers. Eugene Ysaÿe, conductor. Columbia. 1921.

CHABRIER: Marche joyeuse. Eugene Ysaÿe, conductor. Columbia. 1921.

WALTON: Violin Concerto. Jascha Heifetz, violin. Eugene Goossens, conductor. Victor. 1941.

VAUGHAN WILLIAMS: Symphony No. 2. Eugene Goossens, conductor. Victor. 1941.

TCHAIKOVSKY: Symphony No. 2. Eugene Goossens, conductor. Victor. 1941.

GRIEG: Peer Gynt: Suite No. 1. Eugene Goossens, conductor. Victor. 1945.

STRAVINSKY: The Song of the Nightingale. Eugene Goossens, conductor. Victor. 1945.

STRAUSS, RICHARD: Der Rosenkavalier Suite. Eugene Goossens, conductor. Victor. 1945.

CHABRIER: Marche joyeuse. Eugene Goossens, conductor. Victor. 1945.

SCHUMANN: Symphony No. 4. Eugene Goossens, conductor. Victor. 1946.

DELIUS: A Village Romeo and Juliet: Walk to the Paradise Gardens. Eugene Goossens, conductor. Victor. 1946.

RESPIGHI: The Pines of Rome. Eugene Goossens, conductor. Victor. 1946.

BERLIOZ: Les nuits d'été. Suzanne Danco, soprano. Thor Johnson, conductor. Decca. 1951.

ALFVEN: Midsummer Vigil - Swedish Rhapsody. Thor Johnson, conductor. Decca. 1951.

SCHUBERT: Symphony No. 3. Thor Johnson, conductor. London Decca. 1951.

BACH, JOHANN CHRISTIAN: Sinfonia No. 1 in E-flat Major. Thor Johnson, conductor. London Decca. 1951.

GRIEG: Sigurd Jorsalfar Suite. Thor Johnson, conductor. London Decca. 1951.

DVORÁK: Symphony No. 8. Thor Johnson, conductor. Remington. 1953.

SIBELIUS: Origin of Fire. Sulo Saarits, baritone; Helsinki University Chorus; Thor Johnson, conductor. Remington. 1953.

SIBELIUS: Pohjola's Daughter. Thor Johnson, conductor. Remington. 1953.

BRANT: Saxophone Concerto. Sigurd Rascher, saxophone; Thor Johnson, conductor. Remington. 1953.

GERSHWIN: Piano Concerto in F Major. Alec Templeton, piano; Thor Johnson, conductor. Remington. 1953.

PROKOFIEV: Piano Concerto No. 2. Jorge Bolet, piano; Thor Johnson, conductor. Remington. 1954.

TCHAIKOVSKY: Symphony No. 2. Thor Johnson, conductor. Remington. 1954.

STEIN: Three Hassidic Dances. Thor Johnson, conductor. Remington. 1954.

WARD: Symphony No. 3. Thor Johnson, conductor. Remington. 1954

GUTSCHE (GUTCHÉ): Symphony No. 5. Max Rudolf, conductor. CRI. 1964.

PAGANINI: Violin Concerto No. 2. Ruggiero Ricci, violin; Max Rudolf, conductor. Decca. 1965.

SAINT-SAËNS: Violin Concerto No. 1. Ruggiero Ricci, violin; Max Rudolf, conductor. Decca. 1965.

HAYDN: Symphony No. 86. Max Rudolf, conductor. Decca. 1965.

HAYDN: Symphony No. 57. Max Rudolf, conductor. Decca. 1965.

NIELSEN: Maskarade: Overture. Max Rudolf, conductor. Decca. 1966.

NIELSEN: Symphony No. 4. Max Rudolf, conductor. Decca. 1966.

BRAHMS: Symphony No. 4. Max Rudolf, conductor. Decca. 1966.

MOZART: Serenade for Orchestra. K. 320. Eugene Blee, posthorn; George Hambrecht, flautino; Max Rudolf, conductor. Decca. 1966.

MOZART: Symphony No. 28, K. 173e. Max Rudolf, conductor. Decca. 1966.

BRUCKNER: Symphony No. 7. Max Rudolf, conductor. Decca. 1967.

MENDELSSOHN: Symphony No. 5. Max Rudolf, conductor. Decca. 1967.

BERWALD: Symphony No. 5. Max Rudolf, conductor. Decca. 1967.

BEETHOVEN: Symphony No. 3. Max Rudolf, conductor. Decca. 1968.

STRAUSS, RICHARD: Der Rosenkavalier Suite. Max Rudolf, conductor. Decca. 1968.

STRAUSS, JOHANN II: Die Fledermaus: Overture. Max Rudolf, conductor. Decca. 1968.

STRAUSS, JOHANN II: Wine, Women, and Song. Max Rudolf, conductor. Decca. 1968.

STRAUSS, JOHANN II: Thunder and Lightning Polka. Max Rudolf, conductor. Decca. 1968.

BIZET: Symphony No. 1. Max Rudolf, conductor. Decca. 1969.

ROUSSEL: Suite for Orchestra. Max Rudolf, conductor. Decca. 1969.

D'INDY: Ishtar, Symphonic Variations. Max Rudolf, conductor. Decca. 1969.

TCHAIKOVSKY: Symphony No. 6. Max Rudolf, conductor. Decca. 1969.

SCHUMAN: New England Triptych. Max Rudolf, conductor. Decca. 1969.

MENNIN: Canto for Orchestra. Max Rudolf, conductor. Decca. 1969.

WEBERN: Passacaglia for Orchestra. Max Rudolf, conductor. Decca. 1969.

DALLAPICCOLA: Variazoni per orchestra. Max Rudolf, conductor. Decca. 1969.

HAYDN: Symphony No. 91. Max Rudolf, conductor. Decca. 1970.

HAYDN: Symphony No. 102. Max Rudolf, conductor. Decca. 1970.

BRUBECK: The Light in the Wilderness. William Justus, baritone; Miami University a Cappella singers, George Barron, director; Dave Brubeck, piano; Frank Proto, string bass and del rhuba; David Frerichs, jazz drums and tablas; Gerre Hancock, organ; Erich Kunzel, conductor. Decca. 1968.

BRUBECK: The Gates of Justice. Cantor Harold Orbach, tenor; McHenry Boatwright, bass-baritone; Westminster Choir, Robert Carwithen, director; Dave Brubeck Trio (Dave Brubeck, piano and combo organ, Jack Six, bass, Alan Dawson, drums); members of the Philharmonia Orchestra of the University of Cincinnati College-Conservatory of Music; Robert Delcamp, organ; brass ensemble from the Cincinnati Symphony Orchestra; Erich Kunzel, conductor. Decca. 1970.

ELLINGTON: New World A'Coming. Duke Ellington, piano; Erich Kunzel, conductor. Decca. 1970.

ELLINGTON: Harlem. Duke Ellington, piano; Erich Kunzel, conductor. Decca. 1970.

ELLINGTON: The Golden Broom and the Golden Apple. Duke Ellington, piano; Erich Kunzel, conductor. Decca. 1970.

Album entitled: BRUBECK/MULLIGAN/CINCINNATI. Dave Brubeck, piano; Jack Six, bass; Alan Dawson, drums; Gerry Mulligan, baritone saxophone, Erich Kunzel, conductor. Decca. 1971.

MUSSORGSKY: Pictures at an Exhibition. Erich Kunzel, conductor. Decca. 1970

BERLIOZ: Roman Carnival Overture. Erich Kunzel, conductor. Decca. 1970.

BRUBECK: Truth is Fallen. Charlene Peterson, soprano; St. John's Assembly Chorus, Gordon Franklin, director; New Heavenly Blue; Dave Brubeck, piano; Erich Kunzel, conductor. Atlantic. 1972.

ROSSINI: Staber Mater. Sung-Sook Lee, soprano; Florence Quivar, mezzo-soprano; Kenneth Riegel, tenor; Paul Plishka, bass; May Festival Chorus, Thomas Peck, director; Thomas Schippers, conductor. Turnabout. 1976.

STRAUSS, RICHARD: Don Juan. Thomas Schippers, conductor. Turnabout. 1977

STRAUSS, RICHARD: Salome's Dance of the Seven Veils. Thomas Schippers, conductor. Turnabout. 1977

STRAUSS, RICHARD: Der Rosenkavalier Waltzes. Thomas Schippers, conductor. Turnabout. 1977.

STRAUSS, RICHARD: Till Eulenspiegel's Merry Pranks. Thomas Schippers. Turnabout. 1977.

SCHUBERT: Symphony No. 8. Thomas Schippers, conductor. Candide. 1978

SCHUBERT: Symphony No. 9. Thomas Schippers, conductor. Vox/Moss. 1977.

ROSSINI: Semiramide: Overture. Thomas Schippers, conductor. Vox/Moss. 1977.

ROSSINI: Tancredi: Overture. Thomas Schippers, conductor. Vox/Moss. 1977.

ROSSINI: La Gazza Ladra: Overture. Thomas Schippers, conductor. Vox/Moss. 1977.

ROSSINI: La Cenerentola: Overture. Thomas Schippers, conductor. Vox/Moss. 1977.

ROSSINI: William Tell: Overture. Thomas Schippers, conductor. Vox/Moss. 1977.

MENDELSSOHN: A Midsummer Night's Dream (excerpts). Walter Susskind, conductor. Candide. 1978.

SHOSTAKOVICH: Symphony No. 1. Walter Susskind, conductor. Vox/Cum Laude. 1978.

SHOSTAKOVICH: Symphony No. 10. Walter Susskind, conductor. Vox/Cum Laude. 1978.

MAHLER: Das Lied von der Erde. Lili Chookasian, contralto; Richard Cassilly, tenor; Walter Susskind, conductor. Candide/Moss. 1978.

TCHAIKOVSKY: Piano Concerto No. 2. Shura Cherkassky, piano; Walter Susskind, conductor. Vox/Cum Laude. 1978.

MENDELSSOHN: Piano Concerto No. 2. Peter Frankl, piano; John Nelson, conductor. Vox/Moss. 1980.

SCHUMANN: Konzertstück in F Major. John Nelson, conductor. Vox/Moss. 1980.

BEETHOVEN: Symphony No. 3. Michael Gielen, conductor. Vox/Moss. 1980.

BERG: "Lulu" Suite. Kathleen Battle, soprano; Michael Gielen, conductor. Vox/Moss. 1981.

BERG: Lyric Suite. Michael Gielen, conductor. Vox/Moss. 1981.

STRAUSS, RICHARD: Oboe Concerto. Heinz Holliger, oboe; Michael Gielen, conductor. Vox/Moss. 1983.

LUTOSLAWSKI: Double Concerto for Oboe and Harp. Heinz Holliger, oboe; Ursula Holliger, harp; Michael Gielen, conductor. Vox/Moss. 1983.

BUSONI: "Turandot" Suite. Michael Gielen, conductor. Vox/Moss. 1983.

BUSONI: Two Studies from "Doktor Faust." Michael Gielen, conductor. Vox/Moss. 1983.

CARTER: Piano Concerto. Ursula Oppens, piano; Michael Gielen, conductor. New World Records. 1984.

CARTER: Variations for Orchestra. Michael Gielen, conductor. New World Records. 1985.

STRAUSS, RICHARD: Death and Transfiguration. Michael Gielen, conductor. Vox/Moss. 1986.

STRAUSS, RICHARD: Metamorphoses. Michael Gielen, conductor. Vox/Moss. 1986.

DE FALLA: The Three-Cornered Hat (complete). Florence Quivar, mezzo-soprano; Men of the May Festival Chorus; Jesús López-Cobos, conductor. Telarc. 1987.

DE FALLA: Homenajes. Jesús López-Cobos, conductor. Telarc. 1987.

DE FALLA: La Vida Breve: Interlude & Spanish Dance. Jesús López-Cobos, conductor. Telarc. 1987.

RAVEL: Alborado del gracioso. Jesús López-Cobos, conductor. Telarc. 1988.

RAVEL: Rapsodie espagnole. Jesús López-Cobos, conductor. Telarc. 1988.

RAVEL: Valses nobles et sentimantales. Jesús López-Cobos, conductor. Telarc. 1988.

RAVEL: La Valse. Jesús López-Cobos, conductor. Telarc. 1988.

RAVEL: Bolero. Jesús López-Cobos, conductor. Telarc. 1988.

BRUCKNER: Symphony No. 7. Jesús López-Cobos, conductor. Telarc. 1989.

BRUCKNER: Symphony No. 4. Jesús López-Cobos, conductor. Telarc. 1990.

BIZET: Suite from "Carmen." Jesús López-Cobos, conductor. Telarc. 1990.

BIZET: L'arlesienne Suite No. 1. Jesús López-Cobos, conductor. Telarc. 1990.

BIZET: Symphony No. 1. Jesús López-Cobos, conductor. Telarc. 1990.

FRANCK: Symphony in D Minor. Jesús López-Cobos, conductor. Telarc. 1990.

FRANCK: Le Chasseur maudit. Jesús López-Cobos, conductor. Telarc. 1990.

BRUCKNER: Symphony No. 6. Jesús López-Cobos, conductor. Telarc. 1991.

MAHLER: Songs of a Wayfarer. Andreas Schmidt, baritone; Jesús López-Cobos, conductor. Telarc. 1991.

MAHLER: Songs on the Death of Children. Andreas Schmidt, baritone; Jesús López-Cobos, conductor. Telarc. 1991.

MAHLER: Rückert Lieder. Andreas Schmidt, baritone; Jesús López-Cobos, conductor. Telarc. 1991.

BRUCKNER: Symphony No. 9. Jesús López-Cobos, conductor. Telarc. 1992.

DE FALLA: La Vida Breve (complete). Alicia Nafe, Salud; Antonio Ordones, Paco; Jesús López-Cobos, conductor. Telarc. 1992.

BRUCKNER: Symphony No. 8. Jesús López-Cobos, conductor. Telarc. 1993.

RESPIGHI: Church Windows. Jesús López-Cobos, conductor. Telarc. 1993.

RESPIGHI: Brazilian Impressions. Jesús López-Cobos, conductor. Telarc. 1993.

RESPIGHI: Roman Festivals. Jesús López-Cobos, conductor. Telarc. 1993.

WAGNER: Die Meistersinger von Nürnberg: Overture. Jesús López-Cobos, conductor. Telarc. 1994.

WAGNER: Rienzi: Overture. Jesús López-Cobos, conductor. Telarc. 1994.

WAGNER: Faust: Overture. Jesús López-Cobos, conductor. Telarc. 1994.

WAGNER: The Flying Dutchman: Overture. Jesús López-Cobos, conductor. Telarc. 1994.

WAGNER: Tristan and Isolde: Prelude and Liebestod. Jesús López-Cobos, conductor. Telarc. 1994.

WAGNER: Tannhäuser: Overture. Jesús López-Cobos, conductor. Telarc. 1994.

CINCINNATI POPS ORCHESTRA RECORDINGS
Erich Kunzel, Conductor

A Portrait of George. Vox Turnabout
Amen! A Gospel Celebration. Telarc
American as Apple Pie. VoxBox
American Fantasia. Vox Turnabout
American Jubilee. Telarc
American Piano Classics. Telarc
An International Salute. Vox Cum Laude
Big Band Hit Parade. Telarc
Bond & Beyond. Telarc
Casey at the Bat/Peter and the Wolf. Moss Music Group
Chiller. Telarc
Christmas with the Pops. Telarc
Classics of the Silver Screen. Telarc
Copland: Lincoln Portrait/Old American Songs. Telarc
Dances from the Opera. Vox Cum Laude
Disney Spectacular. Telarc
Down on the Farm. Telarc
Ein Straussfest. Telarc
Ein Straussfest II. Telarc
Fantastic Journey. Telarc
Fiesta! Telarc
Gershwin: Rhapsody in Blue/ Concerto in F. Telarc
Gershwin: Rhapsody in Blue/An American in Paris. Telarc
Gershwin: Porgy & Bess/Grofe: Grand Canyon Suite. Telarc
Happy Trails. Telarc
Hollywood's Greatest Hits. Telarc
Hollywood's Greatest Hits, Volume II. Telarc
International Salute. VoxBox
Lerner & Loewe Songbook. Telarc
Mancini's Greatest Hits. Telarc
Movie Love Themes. Telarc
Music Man. Telarc
Music of Waldteufel. Vox Cum Laude
Offenbach: Concerto Rondo for Cello & Orchestra. Vox Turnabout
Offenbach: Gaite Parisienne/Meyerbeer: Les Patineurs. Vox Turnabout
Offenbach: Gaite Parisienne/Ibert: Divertissement. Telarc
Offenbach Overtures. Vox Turnabout
Orchestral Spectaculars. Telarc
Peaches and Cream. Vox Cum Laude
Peter and the Wolf/Tubby the Tuba. Caedmon
Peter and the Wolf/The Ugly Duckling. Moss Music Group
Pomp & Circumstance. Vox Turnabout
Pomp & Pizzaz. Telarc
Pops Plays Puccini. Telarc
Rodgers & Hammerstein Songbook. Telarc
Round-up. Telarc
Sailing. Telarc
Sound of Music. Telarc
Star Tracks. Telarc
Star Tracks II. Telarc
Stokowski Sound. Telarc
Symphonic Spectacular. Telarc
Tchaikovsky: 1812 Overture. Telarc
The Dance. VoxBox
The Fantastic Stokowski. Telarc
The Very Best of Erich Kunzel and the Cincinnati Pops - Top 20. Telarc
Time Warp. Telarc
Trumpet Spectacular. Telarc
Unforgettably Doc. Telarc
Vive La France/The Music of Jacques Offenbach. VoxBox
William Tell/Other Favorite Overtures. Telarc
Victory at Sea. Telarc
Young at Heart. Telarc

**The CSO Centennial Celebration is made possible
by a generous grant from the Trustees of The Corbett Foundation
as a special tribute to its founders,
J. Ralph and Patricia A. Corbett.**

Centennial Celebration Honor Roll
Ames Travel Service, Inc.
Artistic Opportunity Fund of the Cincinnati Institute of Fine Arts
Sam Ashworth Design
Brendamour Warehousing, Moving, Distribution and Services, Inc.
Cincinnati Gas & Electric
Cincinnati Historical Society
Cincinnati Symphony Club
J. Rawson Collins
COMAIR
Martha Harkness Charitable Trust
The Hennegan Company
Lazarus/Federated Dept. Stores, Inc.
Magellan Travel, Inc.
Mercantile Stores Co., Inc.
The Merten Company
Frank Messer & Sons Construction, Inc.
Osborne Coinage Company
Renaissance Investment Management, Inc.
Dr. & Mrs. George Rieveschl, Jr.
RIS Paper Co.
Richard Saunders International
Frieda Schwenkmeyer Charitable Trust
Scripps Howard Inc.
Star Bank
Mr. & Mrs. Joseph Stern, Jr.
University of Cincinnati - College of Design, Architecture, Art & Planning
University of Cincinnati - College Conservatory of Music,
Electronic Media Division

CSO Centennial Celebration Steering Committee
Joyce Holmes, CSO Centennial Celebration Co-Chair
Rosemary Schlachter, CSO Centennial Celebration Co-Chair

Sam Ashworth, Publications Chair
Jan Barclay, CSO Volunteer Administrator
George Blake, Publications
Trish Bryan, Broadcasting/Exhibitions Chair
Cecie Chewning, Centennial Exhibit
Dianne Cooper, CSO Marketing Director
Dianne Dunkelman, Community Celebration
Ora Forusz, Cincinnati Symphony Club Liaison
Eugene Frey, Oral History/Performances
Marcia Gammeter, Special Events Chair
Mary Ghory, Public Relations/Governmental Recognition Chair
Donald Gibson, Oral History
Brian Gillan, Community Celebration Chair
Kenneth Goode, CSO Development Director
Barbara Harshman, Opening Weekend Co-Chair
Dan Hoffheimer, Community Celebration and Board Liaison
Robert Howes, Publications/Archives
Marlene Johnson, Opening Weekend Co-Chair
Mark Kallick, Community Celebration Vice-Chair
Sally Krefting, Public Relations/Marketing
Steven Monder, CSO Executive Director
Nancy Nolan, CSO Public Relations Manager
Bryan Palmer-Smith, Children's Events Chair
Norma Petersen, Reunion Chair
Gale Peterson, Cincinnati Historical Society Liaison
* Sam Pogue, Symposium Chair
Joseph Stern, Publications/Archives
Sue Straus, Opening Weekend Co-Chair/Archives Chair

* Deceased

The Cincinnati Symphony Orchestra would like to thank
all the volunteers who made the Centennial Celebration possible.

BIBLIOGRAPHY

Periodicals

Braine, R. "Eugene Ysaÿe." Etude, October 1931, p. 743.

"Cincinnati Coup: A. Schonberg's Gurre-lieder." Newsweek, February 12, 1951, p. 74.

"Cincinnati hires Rudolf." Woodwind World, December 1957, p.2.

"Cincinnati post goes to Gielen." Billboard, January 20, 1979, pp. 42.

" Circumnavigate globe: believe Cincy symphony first orchestra to do so." Variety, January 26, 1966, p. 47.

"Frank Van der Stucken: Portrait." Music, September 1900, p. 412.

Goossens, Eugene. "Civic worth of a symphony orchestra." Musician, June 1933, p. 4.

"Max Rudolf [bio. port.]" Santa Cecilia, No. 5, 1960 sup, p. 42.

"Migration of Mr. Goossens." Newsweek, December 2, 1946, pp. 99-100.

Pogue, S. F. "Some unpublished letters of Stokowski." Notes, No. 1 1989, pp. 25-36.

"Portrait: Fritz Reiner." Business Week, October 14, 1931, p. 9.

"Rudolf new conductor of CSO." Musical Courier, December 15, 1957, p. 4.

"Schippers' 5th season set with CSO's 80th birthday." Billboard, March 2, 1974, p. 43.

"Stokowski and the Cincinnati Symphony Orchestra, a portrait." Outlook, November 27, 1909, pp. 661-662.

Stokowski, Leopold. "Where does America stand musically as creator, producer & audience?" Craftsman, February 1916, pp. 523-530.

Thomas, Louis R. "Richard II Visits the Queen City." Queen City Heritage 44 (Spring 1986): 37-44.

Thomas, Louis R. "The CSO: Rise and Fall and Rebirth: 1895-1909." Queen City Heritage 42 (Summer 1984): 15-23.

Thomas, Louis R. "Stokowski on Podium." Queen City Heritage 42 (Summer 1984): 25-33.

"Thomas Schippers chiefs Cincinnati." Variety, April 9, 1969, p. 67.

"Thor Johnson: Artists touring abroad." Musical Courier, June 1957, p. 5.

"Thor Johnson-On the Cover." Musical Courier, December 1, 1950.

Printed Works

Cincinnati Music Hall Association. Golden Jubilee: Cincinnati Music Hall, 1878-1928.

Cincinnati Symphony Orchestra: A Tribute to Max Rudolf and Highlights of Its History. Cincinnati: CSO Trustees, 1967.

Fellers, Frederick P. Discographies of Commerical Recordings of the Cleveland Orchestra (1924-1977) and the Cincinnati Symphony Orchestra (1917-1977). Westport, CT: Greenwood Press, 1978.

Ginzburg, Lev Solomonovich. Ysaÿe. Neptune City, NJ: Paganiniana Publications, 1980.

Kowert, Nancy. A Musical Star Over Texas. Fredericksburg, Texas: N. Kowert Publishers, [1963].

Opperby, Preben. Leopold Stokowski. New York: Hippocrene Books, 1982.

Rosen, Carole. The Goossens: A Musical Century. London: Andre Deutsch, Ltd., 1993.

Smith, William A. The Mystery of Leopold Stokowski. Rutherford, NJ: Fairleigh Dickerson University Press, 1990.

Stokowski, Leopold. Music for All of Us. New York: Simon and Schuster, 1943.

Ysaye, Antoine. Ysaÿe. Translated by Frank Clarkson. Great Missenden, Buckinghamshire: W.E. Hill, 1980.

Theses and Dissertations

Thomas, Louis R. "A History of the Cincinnati Symphony Orchestra to 1931." Ph.D. dissertation, University of Cincinnati Department of History, 1972 (2v.).

Thomas, Louis R. "The Cincinnati Symphony Orchestra Under the Direction of Fritz Reiner, 1922-1931." MA thesis, University of Cincinnati, 1963.

Audio Video Tape and Film Archives

British Broadcasting Company (BBC). Basil Moss interview with Leopold Stokowski, 1969.

Journals

Cincinnati Fine Arts Journal. Vol. 1, no. 1 (July 1928) to Vol. 9, no. 5 (Spring 1939). 9 v. illus.

Stumpf, Robert, ed. Maestrino: The Journal of the Leopold Stokowski Society of America. Columbus, OH: 1983 to date.

Toccata: The Journal of the Leopold Stokowski Society. London: March/April 1980 to date.

BIBLIOGRAPHY

Collections and Papers

Cincinnati Symphony Orchestra.
   Children's May Festival under the auspices of the German-American Free Kindergarten Association, 2,000 children's series, selected
   from the public schools of Cincinnati. May 1 and 8, 1897, Frank Van der Stucken, musical director. Cincinnati Public Library.
Cincinnati Symphony Orchestra Association.
   Musicians contracts, seasons of 1923/24 - 1929/30, 1931/32 - 1935/36. Cincinnati Historical Society.
Cincinnati Symphony Orchestra Association.
   News release announcing the death of Music Director Thomas Schippers, dated Cincinnati, December 16, 1977. Cincinnati Historical Society.
Cincinnati Symphony Orchestra Association.
   Newspaper clippings relating to Cincinnati Symphony Orchestra 1902-1964. [Scrapbooks]. 86 vols. Cincinnati Historical Society.
Cincinnati Symphony Orchestra.
   Clipping Files, 1943-1992. Public Library of Cincinnati and Hamilton County
Felton, James.
   Leopold Stokowski Collection, ca. 1853-1970. University of Maryland Library (College Park).
Heintz, Victor E. Papers
   Alien property custodian legal records pertaining to Ernst Kunwald (1922). Cincinnati Historical Society.
Kemper, Willis Miller, 1854-1923.
   Scrapbooks of clippings, broadsides, programs, etc. from Cincinnati cultural events from 1865-1907. Cincinnati Historical Society.
Pogue, Samuel F.
   Papers, 1972-1979. Cincinnati Historical Society.
Wulsin Family Papers, 1820-1981.
   Manuscript material relating to the Wulsin family. Cincinnati Historical Society.

Pamphlets

A half century of golden music, 1894-95 – 1944-45: The story of the CSO. 1945. Cincinnati Historical Society.
Cincinnati Symphony Orchestra. Carnegie Hall Concert of January 9, 1917. Cincinnati Historical Society.
Cincinnati Symphony Orchestra. Complimentary Concert to the members of the Cincinnati Institute of Fine Arts. November 20, 1929.
    Cincinnati Historical Society.
Cincinnati Symphony Orchestra and the Cincinnati Art Club.
   Living Bronzes illustrating the Spanish-American War & Pictures by the great masters by the Cincinnati Art Club, February 21-22, 1899
   for the benefit of the Cincinnati Symphony Orchestra. Cincinnati Historical Society.
Cincinnati Symphony Orchestra and the Cincinnati Art Club.
   Tableaux Vivants given by Cincinnati Art Club, April 23, 1898 for the benefit of the Orchestra Fund. Program. Cincinnati Historical Society.
Cincinnati Symphony Orchestra. "Opening night at the Palace for the benefit of the CSO." Program. 1978. Music Hall, Cincinnati, Ohio.
Cincinnati Symphony Orchestra. Program/Guide. "1990 Far East Tour." 22 October - 20 November, 1990. Music Hall, Cincinnati, Ohio.
Cincinnati Symphony Orchestra. Formation and history of the CSO. 60th anniversary season, booklet and perspective, pp. 10-13. Cincinnati
   Historical Society.
Cincinnati Symphony Orchestra. General Motors Promenade Concert, April 25, 1937. Cincinnati Historical Society.
Cincinnati's Music Hall with essays by Zane L. Miller & George F. Roth with an introduction by Luke Feck. 1978. Cincinnati Historical Society.
Conservatoire Royal de musique de Liege. Centencire de la naissance de Eugene Ysaye. 16 Juillet 1858, 12 Mai 1931, Liege, [France]. Cincinnati
   Historical Society.
German-American Free Kindergarten Association. May 1 & 8, 1897. Frank Van der Stucken, musical director, Cincinnati Historical Society.
Memorial concert, Cincinnati Symphony Orchestra and Cincinnati May Festival Chorus. April 13, 1919. Cincinnati Historical Society.
"Sir Eugene Goossens: The Orchestra Builder." 2MBS-FM Program Guide, May 1993. Music Hall, Cincinnati, Ohio
Special Program in honor of Mr. and Mrs. Charles P. Taft, October 18-19, 1929 at Emery Auditorium. Cincinnati Historical Society.
Symphony concert in honor of the visit of Majesties King Albert and Queen Elizabeth of Belgium, October 22, 1919. Program. Cincinnati
   Historical Society.
Weber, Bertha Henry. "A retrospective panorama of my 25 years with the Women's Committee for the Cincinnati Symphony Orchestra," 1962.
   Cincinnati Historical Society.

CSO Resident Conductors
Associate Conductors
Assistant Conductors

1895	Michael Brand	Assistant Conductor
1895-1924	Ralph Lyford	Associate Conductor
1927-1937	Vladimir Bakaleinikoff	Assistant Conductor
1947-1948	Walter Heerman	Assistant Conductor
1959-1963	Haig Yaghjian	Assistant Conductor
1963-1964	Ronald Ondrejka	Assistant Conductor
1964-1965	Ronald Ondrejka	Associate Conductor'
1965-1967	Erich Kunzel	Assistant Conductor
1967-1968	Erich Kunzel	Associate Conductor
1968-1975	Erich Kunzel	Resident Conductor
	Carmon DeLeone	Assistant Conductor
1975-1976	Carmon DeLeone	Assistant Conductor
	David Stahl	Conducting Assistant
1976-1979	Carmon DeLeone	Resident Conductor
	David Stahl	Exxon/Arts Endowment Conductor
1979-1980	Carmon DeLeone	Resident Conductor
1980-1982	Bernard Rubenstein	Associate Conductor
1982-1986	Bernard Rubenstein	Associate Conductor
	David Loebel	Assistant Conductor
1986-1990	David Loebel	Associate Conductor
1990-1992	Keith Lockhart	Assistant Conductor
1992-Pres.	Keith Lockhart	Associate Conductor
1977-Pres.	Erich Kunzel	Cincinnati Pops Conductor

CSO Managers

1901-1911	Frank E. Edwards
1911-1913	Oscar Hatch Hawley
1913-1918	Kline L. Roberts
1918-1923	A.F. Thiele
1923-1925	Mrs. Jessie W. Darby
1925-1926	Charles Pearson
1926-1930	Roy Hornikel
1930-1936	Stuart M. Thompson
1936-1938	Theo F. Gannon
1938-1943	Edgar Friedlander (Acting Mgr.)
1943-1949	J.M. O'Kane
1949-1951	Robert Casey
1951-1963	Craig Hutchinson
1963-1971	Lloyd H. Haldeman
1971-1975	Albert K. Webster
1975-1976	Kenneth Haas
1976-Pres.	Steven Monder

Presidents of CSO Women's Committee and Cincinnati Symphony Association

1936-1937	Mrs. Frances S. Wyman
1937-1938	Mrs. Alexander Thomson
1938-1939	Mrs. Polk Laffoon
1939-1940	Mrs. Anthony D. Bullock
1940-1941	Mrs. Gordon McKim
1941-1942	Mrs. Albert P. Strietmann
1942-1943	Mrs. Harry W. Randolph
1943-1945	Mrs. Erwin B. Bosworth
1945-1946	Mrs. Cornelius J. Hauck
1946-1947	Mrs. Marion H. Woody
1947-1948	Mrs. Harold R. LeBlond
1948-1949	Mrs. Fred Lazarus III
1949-1950	Mrs. Robert K. Rogan
1950-1951	Mrs. John C. Pogue
1951-1953	Mrs. Roger H. Ferger
1953-1954	Mrs. William E. Greiss
1954-1955	Mrs. Louis Nippert
1955-1956	Mrs. Robert F. Gerwin
1956-1957	Mrs. Robert J. Amidon
1957-1958	Mrs. Joseph G. Poetker
1958-1959	Mrs. Richard R. Deupree
1959-1960	Mrs. William A. Altemeier
1960-1961	Mrs. Paul W. Steer
1961-1962	Mrs. John Z. Herschede
1962-1963	Mrs. Walter C. Langsam
1963-1964	Mrs. Francis W. Eustis
1964-1965	Mrs. Leroy R. Brooks
1965-1966	Mrs. James R. Williams
1966-1967	Mrs. W. Thomas McElhinney
1967-1968	Mrs. Wesley Love
1968-1969	Mrs. Fletcher E. Nyce
1969-1970	Mrs. Timothy D. Hinckley
1970-1971	Mrs. Maurice D. Marsh
1971-1972	Mrs. Philip O.Geier
1972-1973	Mrs. S. Charles Straus
1973-1974	Mrs. Harold L. Holmes
1974-1975	Mrs. Ethan B. Stanley
1975-1977	Mrs. William R. Seaman
1977-1979	Mrs. Gerald C. Petersen
1979-1980	Mrs. James A. Salinger
1980-1981	Mrs. Richard Thayer
1981-1982	Mrs. Rupert A. Doan
1982-1983	Mrs. Charles Fleischmann
1983-1984	Mrs. Joseph E. Ghory
1984-1985	Mrs. Julien E. Benjamin, Jr.
1985-1986	Mrs. Susan S. Stanley
1986-1987	Marlene Rowat
1987-1989	Mrs. Frederick E. Bryan III
1989-1991	Rosemary Schlachter
1991-1992	H. Spencer Liles
1992-1994	Barbara Harshman
1994-1995	Sally Krefting

Presidents and Chairmen of Cincinnati Symphony Orchestra Board

1895-1900	Mrs. William H. Taft - President
1900-1913	Mrs. Christian R. Holmes - President
1913-1929	Mrs. Charles P. Taft - President
1929-1936	Herbert G. French - Chairman
1936-1959	Lucien Wulsin - Chairman
1950-1957	Walter C. Beckjord - President
1957-1961	John R. Bullock - President
1959-1961	Paul W. Christensen - Chairman
1961-1963	Roger H. Ferger - Chairman
1963-1965	Joseph B. Hall - Chairman
1961-1965	Frank T. Hamilton - President
1965-1968	J. Ralph Corbett - Chairman
	Laurence L. Davis - President
1968-1971	Lucien Wulsin, Jr. - Chairman
	John S. Lillard - President
1971-1975	Edgar J. Mack, Jr. - Chairman
	Thomas J. Klinedinst - President
1975-1978	William Beckett - Chairman
	Frank H. Stewart - President
1978-1981	Frank H. Stewart - Chairman
	David J. Joseph, Jr. - President
1981-1984	David J. Joseph, Jr. - Chairman
	James M. Ewell - President
1984-1986	James M. Ewell - Chairman
1984-1987	Charles F. Yeiser - President
1987-1988	Donald J. Stone - President
1988-1991	James R. Bridgeland, Jr. - President
1991-1993	Clement L. Buenger - President
1993-1995	Stephen P. Donovan, Jr. - President

CSO Trustees Since 1895

Robert H. Allen
Mrs. Frederick H. Alms
Mrs. William A. Altemeier
Mrs. Robert J. Amidon
Mrs. Louise Anderson
Charles W. Anness
George W. Armstrong, Jr.
Mrs. Levi A. Ault
William T. Bahlman, Jr.
Charles M. Barrett
William Baskett III
Bertha Baur
James W. Baxter
John W. Beatty
William Beckett
Walter C. Beckjord
Mrs. Albert J. Bell
Mrs. Julien E. Benjamin, Jr.
Theodore M. Berry
Mrs. Gustav Billing
Mrs. William Blaine
Herbert R. Bloch, Jr.
Vincent Bolling, Jr.
Eugene Bonelli
Dennis Brenckle
James R. Bridgeland, Jr.
LeRoy R. Brooks
Mrs. LeRoy R. Brooks
Fred I. Brown
Mrs. Frederick E. Bryan
Clement L. Buenger
John M. Bullock
John R. Bullock
H. E. Burns
Donald L. Caldera
Mrs. Charles O. Carothers
Lee A. Carter
Albert H. Chatfield
Mrs. Albert H. Chatfield
Frederick Chatfield
William H. Chatfield
Oreson H. Christensen
Paul W. Christensen
Raymond R. Clark
A. Burton Closson, Jr.
Thomas C. Cody
Calvin H. Conliffe
J. Ralph Corbett
Mrs. J. Ralph Corbett
W. Howard Cox
Mrs. Briggs Cunningham
Charles E.Curran III
Francis L. Dale
Laurence L. Davis
Mrs. Richard R. Deupree
Norman Dinerstein
Mrs. Rupert Doan
Dorothy Dobbins
Stephen P. Donovan, Jr.
Roger Drackett
Mrs. Charles Duhme
Mrs. Dianne Dunkelman
Richard H. Durrell
Mrs. Frederick Eckstein, Jr.
John J. Emery
Mrs. Arthur Espy
Francis Eustis
James M. Ewell
Mrs. Frederick Exton, Jr.
Anne E. Fehring
Roger Ferger
Mrs. Roger H. Ferger
Mrs. Charles F. Fleischmann
Julius Fleischmann
Kingston Fletcher

Mrs. Frederick Forchheimer
Gerald R. Francis
William M. Freedman
Mrs. J. Walter Freiberg
Maurice Freiberg
Herbert G. French
Alfred J. Friedlander
Edgar Friedlander
Susan Friedlander
William A. Friedlander
Charles M. Fullgraf
Merri Gaither-Smith
Mrs. John Gates
Frederick W. Geier
Mrs. Philip O. Geier
Mrs. Robert F. Gerwin
Mrs. Joseph E. Ghory
John J. Gilligan
Robert D. Gordon
P. Martin Graves
Joseph S. Graydon
Mrs. William E. Griess
Willard G. Grueneberg
Jerry A. Grundhofer
Ateo L. Gulino
William R. Gurganus
Mrs. Adolf Hahn
Lloyd H. Haldeman
Joseph B. Hall
Mrs. Marshall Halstead
Mrs. Robert Halstead
Frank T. Hamilton
John W. Hanley
Mary Hanna
Irving Harris
Mrs. Morton Harshman
Mrs. Cornelius Hauck
Mrs. John Z. Herschede
Mrs. Timothy Hinckley
Donald R. Hinkley
Frederic C. Hirons
Joseph W. Hirschhorn
Charles F. Hofer
Mrs. Charles F. Hofer
Daniel Hoffheimer
Mrs. C. R. Holmes
Mrs. Harold L. Holmes
Dwane Houser
Dett P. Hunter
Mrs. William Ittmann
Earnest L. James
Mrs. F. D. Jamison
Isabel Jelke
E. Eugene Jemail
Richard Jensen
David J. Joseph Jr.
Malcolm Jozoff
Mr. Arthur Judson
Louis E. Kahn
Lawrence A. Kane, Jr.
William J. Keating
Lorrence Kellar
James D. Kiggen
Christopher Kinard
Thomas J. Klinedinst
Robert Knauf
Mrs. R. A. Koehler
George J. Kral
Miss Krippendorf
Mrs. Hugo L. Kupferschmid
Susan S. Laffoon
Mrs. Walter C. Langsam
Mrs. Elizabeth K. Lanier
William M. Lawarre
Mrs. Fenton Lawson

Ralph Lazarus
Mrs. Fred Lazarus III
Mrs. Harold R. Leblond
Mrs. R. K. Leblond
Frank Leister
Lawrence A. Leser
Peter Levin
Charles B. Levinson
Robert Levinson
Harry M. Levy
William N. Liggett
H. Spencer Liles
John S. Lillard
Carl Lindner
John A. Lloyd
Phillip C. Long
Edgar H. Lotspeich
Mrs. Wesley Love
Clara Lukenheimer
Edgar J. Mack Jr.
Elliot Marcus
Mrs. Maurice D. Marsh
Mrs. Lawrence Maxwell, Jr.
Manuel D. Mayerson
Mrs. W. Thomas McElhinney
Mrs. William McD. Kite
Charles S. Mechem, Jr.
Honorable Henry Meigs
Robert L. Miles
James M. E. Mixter
John H. More
Louis T. More
Howard J. Morgens
Mrs. James Morrison
David W. Motch
John T. Murphy
Mrs. Joseph S. Neave
Betsy Kyte Newman
Thomas Nies
Mrs. Louis Nippert
Mrs. Fletcher E. Nyce
James P. Orr
John A. Parlin III
John E. Pepper
Mrs. Gerald C. Petersen
Bradford E. Phillips
Mrs. Lewis F. Phipps
Harold F. Poe
Mrs. Joseph G. Poetker
J. Crawford Pogue, Jr.
Mrs. John C. Pogue
Samuel F. Pogue
Mrs. Lawrence Poland
Joseph W. Polisi
Lee Etta Powell
William Cooper Procter
William M. Ramsey
Frederick Rauh
C. Lawson Reed, Jr.
James B. Reynolds
George Rieveschl, Jr.
Yvonne Robertson
Emma L. Roedter
Roger Kemper Rogan
Mrs. Roger Kemper Rogan
Edward A. Rowat
Marlene Rowat
Brian Rowe
John J. Rowe
William S. Rowe
Mrs. James A. Salinger
Allen Sapp
Robert Schiff
Rosemary K. Schlachter
Louis F. Schlueter

Jacob G. Schmidlapp
W. Kesley Schoepf
Fred O. Schulz
Mrs. William R. Seaman
Edward H. Selonick
James B. Selonick
Mrs. William T. Semple
Frederic C. Shadley
Henry Shaw
Amy Sherlock
A. Clifford Shinkle
Mrs. A. Clifford Shinkle
Mrs. Murray M. Shoemaker
Mrs. Walter K. Sibbald
Donald C. Siekmann
Mrs. Edmund K. Stallo
Robert N. Stargel
Mrs. Paul W. Steer
Thomas Stegman
Joseph S. Stern, Jr.
Frank H. Stewart
Mrs. Louis N. Stix
Alexander Stolley
Donald J. Stone
Peter Strange
Mrs. S. Charles Straus
David S. Swanson
J. Mack Swigert
Charles P. Taft
Mrs. Charles P. Taft
Robert A. Taft
Robert A. Taft Jr.
Mrs. William H. Taft
David E. Taylor
Mrs. Richard Thayer
Rt. Rev. Herbert B. Thompson Jr.
Jay Thompson
Morley P. Thompson
Mrs. Peter G. Thomson
N. Beverley Tucker, Jr.
Smith H. Tyler Jr.
C. William Verity, Jr.
Oliver W. Waddell
Dr. Donald R. Waldrip
Ronald F. Walker
Mrs. Thomas E. Walker
Mrs. George H. Warrington
John W. Warrington
Dr. Jack M. Watson
Sanford G. Weiner
Robert J. Werner
William G. Werner
Charles Westheimer
Harry M. Whipple
Mrs. Frank B. Wiborg
Robert C. Wiegand
Joseph Wilby
Mrs. Joseph Wilby
George J. Wile
Mrs. James R. Williams
Mrs. Marion H. Woody
Frank Wood, Sr.
Sarah H. Woolley
Douglas Workman
Dr. John W. Worrel
Clifford B. Wright
Mrs. Clifford B. Wright
Eugene Wulsin
Lucien Wulsin
Lucien Wulsin, Jr.
B. John Yeager
Charles F. Yeiser
William H. Zimmer
James M. Zimmerman

Cincinnati Symphony Orchestra
Cover and title page; page 6; page 8; page 12, bottom left; page 17, all; pages 18 and 19; page 21, all; pages 22 and 23; page 25, all; page 26, bottom; page 27, middle and bottom; page 28, bottom; page 29, bottom left, bottom right; pages 30 and 31; page 32; pages 34 and 35; page 36, bottom left and right; page 37, middle center and left, bottom left; page 38, top, middle and bottom; page 40, all; page 41, top left both, bottom left both; pages 42 and 43; page 44 through 48; page 49, bottom; page 50, 51 and 52, all; page 53, all except photo; pages 54 through 57; page 61, all; page 62, all; page 63, bottom left and right; page 64, all; page 65, top; page 66 and 67; pages 69, 70 and 71; page 72 and 73, bottom; page 72, top left; page 73, top left, middle and right; page 74, bottom left; page 76, top left, middle, right, bottom left and right; page 77, all; pages 78 and 79; page 81; pages 82 and 83; page 84, all; page 86, top and bottom; page 87, top left, middle left and center, bottom left; page 89, all; pages 90 through 93; page 96, all; page 97, bottom; page 98, bottom left; page 99, top right and left, bottom left; page 100, all; page 101, bottom left and right; pages 102 through 107; page 108, middle center, bottom; page 109, bottom left; pages 110 and 111; page 112, top right, bottom right; page 113, middle left; pages 114 through 119; page 120, top, bottom left; page 121, top left and right; page 124, all; page 125, top, middle right; pages 126 through 133; page 132, bottom; page 134, top; page 136, middle right, bottom right; page 137, top left and right; pages 138 through 145, all; pages 148 and 149, all.

Cincinnati Enquirer
Page 29, top; page 41, top right; pages 58, 59 and 60; page 75; page 85, bottom; page 86, middle; page 88; page 97, top; page 98, top, bottom right; page 99, bottom right; page 108, top left, center and right; page 109, top, middle, bottom right; page 112, top left, middle, bottom left; page 113, top, middle right; page 120, bottom right; page 121, bottom; pages 122 and 123, all; page 125, bottom left; page 133, top; page 133, all; page 134, bottom; page 135; page 136, left;page 137, bottom.

Cincinnati Historical Society
Page 10, all; page 11, all; page 12, top, middle, middle right, bottom right; page 13; page 14, all; page 15; page 20; page 24, all; page 26, photo; page 37, top and middle right; page 65, bottom; page 80; page 85, top; page 94 and 95; page 101, top.

Culver Pictures
Page 28, left; page 29, bottom middle; page 32; page 36, top; page 41, middle right; page 49, top; page 53, photo; page 63, top; page 68; page 72, top right; page 77, center photo; page 87, top right.

Library of Congress
Page 74, right.

Pamela S. Brown
Page 39, top and bottom.

Steven Monder
Pages 146 and 147, all.

Cincinnati Opera
Page 113, bottom.